ADVENTURES IN WINE

ADVENTURES IN WINE

LEGENDS · HISTORY · RECIPES

BY ROBERT LAWRENCE BALZER

edited by ANNA MARIE PETERSON

photographs by the Author

The Ward Ritchie Press

BOOKS BY ROBERT LAWRENCE BALZER:

California's Best Wines
Beyond Conflict
The Pleasures of Wine
Adventures in Wine

CONTENTS

BETWEEN THESE LINES . . .

. . . An Acknowledgment

JACQUES CASANOVA: *Make voyages! Attempt them.*
There's nothing else.

"Camino Real" — Tennessee Williams

THE TWO-LINE dedication from Tennessee Williams' philosophical drama, "Camino Real", might, at first glance seem esoteric to a point of vague irrelevance. In knowing fact, it is more than *sequitur* to the purpose of these generic portrait-studies of wine. Each opens the door to expanding adventures in the realm of taste. The richness of living, the texture of our time, is woven from what we *will* to have it be, beyond chance. Wise or foolish, extravagant or prudent, reckless or provident, "our little life is rounded with a sleep." The day, the hour, the instant we recognize the privilege of personal choice "to make voyages", life seems less arduous, its riddle less depressing. Even if "there is nothing else" this implies almost more than one lifetime can grasp; it is an abundance of pleasure. We establish our own limitations, but as easily as changing thought, we can open the door through those self-built walls. In the seductive charm of wine is an invitation to explore, to adventure with wine.

Along the wine trail, you will meet many others dedicated to this pursuit, who have found it a valid way of life. Between the lines which follow, are the unexpressed dimensions of personal experience which have enriched the author's life. These paragraphs bow, in gratitude, to the many who have contributed in friendship, as Tennessee Williams, to an awareness making life a more joyous adventure.

The name André L. Simon is a legend to many, but to those who have had the privilege of his friendship, it is an unceasing inspiration. Like all men of true greatness, his role as a teacher-by-living-example, reveals a disarming simplicity. No more erudite scholar of the gentle arts of civilization has spanned the 19th and 20th centuries with as much grace and wisdom. The international Wine and Food Society is a living testament to his gospel of good living. Those who attempt to impose rules upon it, have never understood its essence. Those who find it as the passport to new adventure know the heart of André L. Simon.

As Americans, and particularly Californians, we are indebted to the career of Dr. Maynard A. Amerine of the University of California's important College of Viticulture and Enology. Dr. Amerine's role, with that of his associates, in achieving world leadership in the allied sciences of grape-growing and winemaking assists today's and tomorrow's quest for better wines from more suitable acres to satisfy our thirsty demand which will only increase with time.

Time and space telescope the boundaries of friendship-in-wine. Beyond these listed, are many more, but we offer especial gratitude to Claude Taittinger of Reims, Baron Philip Rothschild of Bordeaux, Baron Geoffrey von Mumm of Johannisberg, Barone Luigi Ricasole of Siena, Marchese Niccolo Antinori of Florence, the Viscount de Almocaden of Jerez, and in our homeland, Otto E. Meyer and Stanford Jean Wolf of Paul Masson Vineyards, Brother Timothy, Alfred Fromm, and Otto Sichel of Christian Brothers, the Marquise Helene de Pins and André Tchelistcheff of Beaulieu Vineyards, Louis M. Martini and his son, Louis P. Martini of St. Helena, Eleanor and Frederick McCrea of Stony Hill, Janie and Jack Davies of Schramsberg Vineyards, Peter Mondavi of Charles Krug, Robert Mondavi of Oakville, Lee Stewart of Souverain, Adolph, Paul, and Ben Heck of Korbel, Edith, Ernest, and Karl Wente of Livermore, Joseph Concannon Jr., of Livermore, Antonia and Frank Bartholomew, Al Brett, and Vernon Underwood of Buena Vista, Mr. and Mrs. Douglas Day of Hanzell Vineyards, Eleanor and Martin Ray of Saratoga, H. Peter Jurgens of Almadén Vineyards, Irene and Mike Elwood, and their son Richard, of Mission San Jose, John Daniel of Inglenook Vineyards, the Ficklin family of Madera in the San Joaquin Valley, Douglas Bagier, Norman Mangini, Joseph Walsh, Clem Collette, Ty Jurras, James Willett, and Harold Jurgensen of Los Angeles, Louis Gomberg of San Francisco, Marge Velardo and Robert Nichols of Bullock's in Santa Ana, Carl and Ava Astaire Bostelman of Beverly Hills.

To Anna Marie Peterson, to whose dynamic editorial will, passengers aboard many of today's airlines owe the presence of literary and pictorial reading material, beyond trade house-organs, is owed the initiation of the in-flight magazine. "Flightime," currently aboard PSA, Continental, Aloha, and several other carriers, was the brain-child of Mrs. Peterson. It saw the first appearance of a series of wine-articles by this author, at her direction. We gratefully acknowledge her permission and assistance in bringing those articles within the covers of this book.

Robert Lawrence Balzer

Santa Ana, California
June 1969

ADVENTURES IN WINE

HEART OF THE GRAPE

WHAT IS LIFE? Any answer to this simple question is springboard to definition which cannot stop short of philosophy, for in its fullness it goes beyond "animate existence" to draw in those outward manifestations of living which we call civilization. "*Wine,*" according to the late Ernest Hemingway, "*is one of the most civilized things in the world and one of the natural things of the world that has been brought to the greatest perfection, and it offers a greater range for enjoyment and appreciation than possibly any other purely sensory thing which may be purchased.*"

We have suddenly filled in one arc in the golden round of full definition. In this span called civilization is the joyous evidence of man's living production called wine. It began with Noah when "he planted a vineyard ... and he drank of the Wine." (Genesis 9: 20, 21) It has continued through each recorded civilization. But it depends not wholly upon the living, renewing cycle of the vine, which holds a life of its own, but upon "*the principle or power which is the source or controlling factor of the vital phenomena characteristic of organized beings*" ... which is Webster's primary, unabridged answer to our leading question. *Thus* we find the heart of the grape flowing into its civilized chalice through the direction of man's dynamic energy. The drama of every harvest is never an unvarying repetition of an old vine, but ever a new expression of known elements in new combination ... the land, the vine, its roots, tendrils, fruit, sun, wind, and rain ... man's planting, tending, harvest, pressing, fermentation, patient watching, tasting, aging, bottling.

Every ounce of wine spilling into the bowl of your glass has embraced the full measure of this complex definition of life. It is the taste of civilization. The heart of the grape is man's desire to make wine ... for himself and his fellowman. In reprise, one of man's most civilized products ... is wine. It was true in Persia, in Egypt, in Greece, in Rome, extending into Britain. California's own history began formally when the overland colonizing Spaniards planted, in one ceremony, the Cross, the sword, and the vine, in San Diego, in 1769.

"What is past ... is prologue." To know the best of California wine country, an acquaintance with its men of legend adds a rich dimension to the visual landscape which escapes the casual tourist. It is the aura of history; today is only what it is because of yesterday. In each of

3

California's vineyard valleys, are ghosts of giant men whose monuments are in the heritage of continuing wines and vines . . . General Vallejo Count Haraszthy, Jack London, and Ambassador Zellerbach in Sonoma, Capt. Gustav Niebaum, Jacob Schram, Robert Louis Stevenson, Charles Krug, and Georges de Latour of the Napa Valley, the Wente and Concannon families of Livermore, Korbel of the Russian River, and Paul Masson of the Santa Clara Valley. We can move in their steps, find the tracery of their lives, still living. It cannot help but enhance the pleasure rising from the bowl of your wine-glass. It begins in San Diego and follows El Camino Real north to Sonoma, which lies but an hour of freeway ribbon north of the Golden Gate Bridge. You can take a day, a week, a month, or years, and you will not exhaust the storehouses of romantic history which are background to present vineyard properties. Nowhere else in California does yesterday converge upon today with such dramatic impact as in its vineyards. You are welcome to visit the wineries and taste the product; more than one hundred thousand tourists each year are clocked through the tasting rooms of one Napa Valley Winery, the Victorian-Gothic Greystone Cellars of Christian Brothers, in St. Helena.

Autumn, winter, spring, or summer the wine country is exciting to the sensitive traveler, his camera's eye, his mind's appetite, and his palate's satisfaction. For these reasons, plus years of friendship, I go to the wine countries of California whenever time allows.

Another question is pertinent. *What is wine?*

To say that it is the fermented juice of freshly gathered grapes is not enough. What grapes? What land? Each little globe of nectar with 80 percent of earth-filtered rainfall, has, beyond its own grape sugar, molecular components, which in the miracle of genetic nature, create those differences of taste which are apparent to the most untrained palate. Three fruit-stand varieties of table grapes will tell you how different a Muscat is from a Concord or a Thompson Seedless! Wine grapes, with pedigrees going back to ancient Persia, are boundless in their own variety, and capricious in their transformation into wine. The powdery bloom which covers the skin of each berry is a microscopic dust containing infinite *saccharomycetes*, natural yeast cells, which, when crushed into the blood of the grape, split the atoms of grape sugar in the process we call fermentation. Grape juice becomes wine. In this transformation of grape sugar into alcohol, one co-product is carbon dioxide. Released from open fermenting tanks, it makes the air of wine countries redolent, heady, exciting. Imprisoned in the fermenting wine, it becomes the bubbles in champagne! Some

4

winemakers produce the bubbly beverage in individual stoppered bottles, with enormous care and expense, and others, in large, pressure-controlled stainless steel bulk tanks, at greatly reduced cost, and some change in the final product.

We know that the blood of the Cabernet Sauvignon grape differs from that of the Pinot Noir, or the Zinfandel, Semillon, or Sauvignon Blanc. The Johannisberg Riesling, native to the German Rhineland, is happier in cool regions, whereas the Tinta Madeira, Touriga, and Souzão of Portugal thrive in California's hot central climates. There must be wisdom in planting the correct grape in its proper environment. There must be patience in waiting four years for a measurable harvest, and another two for a minimal testing of the wine. Wine pioneering requires viticultural knowledge, paternal patience, and abundant financing. Beyond this, and of supreme importance, the discipline and drive of the creative artist who knows his objective before it is attained. Such men are few. These are the giants of the wine country, the aristocracy of the soil, the masters of the premium wineries of our State, and of all the celebrated wines of the world. They know what wine is . . . and from the blood of the grape, comes their rich answer to living.

The first commercial vineyard in the Napa Valley was planted in 1850. Wine is still being made in the pioneer locations of Charles Krug, Inglenook, Beringer, and Beaulieu. I have known four generations at this latter "beautiful place" and recently confronted three generations at once in the dynamic Louis M. Martini winery. But the challenge of winemaking is not arrested by entrenched dynasties. There are young vineyards, young winemakers.

Three miles south of Calistoga, a dirt road twists through dense undergrowth, its deep shade from towering redwoods and madrone, shot with filtered shafts of sunlight. It is primitive country. It is alive with deer, rabbit, and great flocks of birds, all beautiful, but menacing to the young vineyards towards which the rustic road rises from the floor of the valley. More than a century ago, a German immigrant from the Rhineland, cut this road to a vineyard site, hired Chinese coolies to dig tunnels into the hillsides, and made wines which were celebrated in lordly London clubs. He was Jacob Schram. Here he was host to Robert Louis Stevenson in 1880. The report of that famous visit in "Silverado Squatters" is more than a treasury of California wine-lore. It is literature that boldly etches the worth of our soil's wine treasure . . . "Those lodes *and pockets of earth, more precious than the precious ores, that yield inimitable fragrance and soft fire; those virtuous*

Bonanzas, where the soil has sublimated under sun and stars to something finer, and the wine is bottled poetry." Stevenson was writing of the Schramberger wines. When Jacob died, the glory of his wines died with him and the property came into ownership lacking the vintage quest. Two youngsters from Southern California, Janie and Jack Davies, trampled out several vintages in another of the State's wine counties, felt deeply the lure of winemaking, purchased the Schram property, cleared out the old vine areas, announced goals of making Schramsberg wines live again. They determined the land, the vines, and the wines . . . Schramsberg Champagne will be of Chardonnay, and Pinot Noir . . . 75 acres of the 150 will also hold Pinot Blanc and some Gamay. The most extensive tunnels in the Napa Valley already hoard a wealthy tirage of bottle-fermented Champagne. There is their first vintage . . . *Reserve Cuvée 1965*, and two more from the subsequent harvest . . . *Vintage 1966* and a unique, delicately salmon-colored *Schramsberg Cuvée de Gamay.* The mountain vaults, which carry the bronze Landmark of the State Historical Society, have begun a new life. Two happier people than Janie and Jack Davies could not be found. Their young sons have a playground that is beyond any backyard of either San Francisco or Pasadena which their parents abandoned in their decision to quit the city existence to follow the wine trail.

Advertising executive Frederick McCrea of San Francisco, and his wife Eleanor, made the same decision a few years ago, and have made their Stony Hill Vineyard, a few ridges distant, a name of esteem to connoisseurs, who make up a waiting list for each vintage of Pinot Chardonnay. We tasted three . . . 1960 and 1962 and 1963. Each was indisputably an outstanding wine, its Chardonnay breed eloquently present, but each was different even to the eye. One was golden, one a pale platinum, and the third, a bright silver. To the taste, each was dry as gun flint . . . *piérre á fusil!*

All years are good in California, but just as weather records are seldom identical, neither are the products of the vine and cellar. In these differences is more than the heart of the grape. Here is the complex wonder which makes wine-lore the subject of poetic conversations that can occupy hours of gentle time. No other beverage is so provocative.

At luncheon, with Brother Timothy of Christian Brothers, we lined up six bottlings of his prize-winning Cabernet Sauvignon, as he demmonstrated his thesis of bottle-age. Time tempers the fruity fragrance of fresher, younger-bottled examples, to a deep cellar velour with passing years. But the surprise was his golden Chateau La Salle, a white wine I had not tasted in several years. It tasted like a bunch of cold, sweet-ripe grapes being crushed right into my mouth.

"You see," Brother Tim said, "time teaches us better ways to make the same wine. It *is* a better wine than the one you remember." Then we tasted his Chenin Blanc, discovering unique delicacy in the opulence of its bouquet.

Standing in the prodigous dimensions of the Louis Martini Winery, where mountains of cased, aging wine stand in square, silent, towering storage, I knew that even this apparent abundance was not enough to fill the demand for these premium wines. For thirty years, I've known those wines, sold them, tasted them, made friends with them and through them. Louis M. Martini is today's Dean of the wine industry. Louis P., his son, already wears the mantle of Master winemaker, and is a strong community leader.

On the western edge of the Napa Valley, at Oakville, is the newest of the county's prestige wineries, handsomely established in the center of its vine-covered acres. It is the Robert Mondavi Winery, designed by Cliff May with a contemporary nod to our Spanish yesterday. Inside the thick, temperature-insulated walls, is the sophisticated and expensive hallmark of winemaking in today's quality control techniques through stainless steel. White wines rest in glass-lined, cooled storage, preserving the brilliance of their crystal personna. Red wines rest in oak, softening the harsh edges of their character, breathing through the pores of the wood. As a member of one of the Napa Valley wine families, Robert grew up in the traditions of wine-making, and now has his own territory to command. It was increased by 250 acres this year, with the acquisition of the long respected Tokalon Vineyards, adjacent to the initial Robert Mondavi vineyard. The first proud wines are just now coming to market under Robert's label . . . a Chenin Blanc, Fumé Blanc, a dry Sauvignon Blanc, and Cabernet Sauvignon.

These few paragraphs can only fragment the Napa Valley story, or serve to incite independent research. The ambitious winelover who strikes off the main trail, will find some worthy treasures at the Souverain Vineyard. And there are others in such premium status: Beaulieu, Beringer, Christian Brothers, Inglenook, Hans Cornell, Heitz, Charles Krug, Louis Martini, Mayacamas, Robert Mondavi, Souverain, Schramsberg, and Stony Hill.

At table with three generations of the founder of Beaulieu, Helene de Pins, her daughter, Dagmar Sullivan, and granddaughter, Paula Sullivan, we listened to winemaker André Tchelisteheff musingly reflect the growth of knowledge brought by years to enhance the glass of wine we were drinking.

"We have returned from the technology of wine-making, to its own philosophy. For a while we replaced art with science . . . scientific research taught us much, but now we have replaced science with individual imagination. Imagination can become lost in the scientific process, but not when there are deep feelings of love. There is no love unless there is imagination . . . and no imagination without love."

The subtle perfection of Beaulieu wines is not an artistic accident. Careful nurturing . . . mark the words . . . make wines greater . . . in this lesson of loving life.

The power of the mind to think, to feel, and will . . . is background to the tranquility that unites the winemaker and his vineyard. The perfection of his product is the wholeness of his philosophy of living. His wine that you can share, may be a silent sermon from the heart of the grape.

. . . There is life in the seed.

Vineyards crown the crest of the mountain ridge which divides the Napa and Sonoma valleys. Cobblestones from one of them, the Goldstein Vineyard of the '90's, were used to pave the steep hills of San Francisco. When he acquired it half a century later, Louis Martini renamed it *Monte Rosso* because of its red volcanic soil.

Moving into the gentle rolling landscape of Sonoma will have rich meaning to those who find the monuments left by the figures who turned this territory into their homeland. All led dramatic lives. The chronicles of their days are California history.

"Dear My-Woman," Jack London wrote to his Chairman, on the fly-leaf of his latest novel when the first copy came from the publisher. *"This is our 'Book of Love' here in our 'Valley of the Moon' where we have lived and known our love ever since that day you rode with me to the divide of the Napa Hills — ay, and before that, before that."* Already one of the most celebrated American novelists, "The Call of the Wild" and "The Sea Wolf" having appeared ten years before, London's new book, "The Valley of the Moon" made lasting and world renowned, this poetic name for that vale of seven moons, the Sonoma Valley, which lies but a brief hour's drive north from the Golden Gate Bridge.

"I would rather be ashes than dust! I would rather that my spark should burn out in a brilliant blaze than it should be stifled by dryrot. I would rather be a superb meteor, every atom of me in magnificent glow, than a sleepy and permanent planet. The proper function of

man is to live, not to exist. I shall not waste my days in trying to prolong them. I shall use my time."

And he did. Few men have lived fuller lives. It is fifty years since his death, but his reality will never die. Nor will the lure of the land where his ashes lie.

To his sister, Eliza Shepard, long entrusted with the supervision of this 1,400-acre domain of tree-clad, vine-robed volcanic Sonoma earth, he wrote an equally emotional dedication in "The Valley of the Moon": "*We know where lies the Valley of the Moon, you and I; and the Valley of the Moon, in our small way, yours and mine, will be a better place for our having been. Your loving brother, Jack London . . . The Ranch . . . Glen Ellen . . . March 7, 1914.*"

His widow wrote about him, pouring over "legal page to legal page" of "musty abstracts" tracing the title to the lands in the Valley of the Moon he had acquired. He wrote: "*Fill your glass and let us look at the parchments of the dreamers of yesterday who dreamed their dreams on your own warm hills.*" On them, he mused about his own extravagant reforestation projects at Beauty Ranch, "*I have scrawled myself with half a hundred thousand eucalyptus trees.*"

They are growing straight and strong and tall today, near the volcanic-stone skeletal remains of Wolf House, his dream mansion which was destroyed by vandal fire within days of its completion, in 1913.

Charmian London built another stone house which is, today, the museum of the Jack London Historical State Park. In this home of rough native stone, "The House of Happy Walls", are the significant and numerous mementoes of London's vigorous, richly varied life . . . the Student, the Socialist, Prince of the Oyster Pirates, the Sailor on Horseback, for the romantic who sailed the seas, came home to ride his own acres as a scientific farmer, an intimate friend of Luther Burbank, who also had stalked deep African jungles with Martin Johnson.

This novelist who wrote stories of violence about the brutality of men, was simultaneously a sensitive creature communing with poet Edwin Markham, stumping as a card-carrying Socialist for his fellow man.

His self-styled "Confession" makes him less a radical than a philosopher in today's light: "I was born in the working class. I early discovered enthusiasm, ambition, and ideals; and to satisfy these became the problem of my childlife. My environment was crude and

9

rough and raw. I had no outlook, but an uplook rather. My place in society was at the bottom. Here life offered nothing but sordidness and wretchedness, both of the flesh and the spirit; for here flesh and spirit were alike, starved and tormented. Above me towered the colossal edifice of society, and to my mind the only way out was up. Into this fabric I early resolved to climb. Up above men wore black clothes and boiled shirts, and women dressed in beautiful gowns.

"Also, there were good things to eat, and there was plenty to eat. This much for the flesh. Then there were the things of the spirit. Up above me, I knew, were unselfishness of the spirit, clean and noble thinking, keen intellectual living. I retain my belief in the nobility and excellence of the human. I believe that spiritual sweetness and unselfishness will conquer the gross gluttony of today. And last of all, my faith is in the working class. As some Frenchwoman has said, 'The stairway of Time is ever echoing with the wooden shoe going up, the polished boot descending.' "

A voracious reader, London attributed much of his own literary success to an early devotion to Ouida's "Signa" and Herbert Spencer's "Philosophy of Style" concerned particularly with the transmission of beauty by words from writer to reader. Scrawled firmly, but legibly in one of his reading notebooks at The Ranch, I noted: *Happiness is the object of existence.* He had found it in the Valley of the Moon . . . the place of his heart's content.

There were two other men of legend when Jack London first arrived in Sonoma, in the autumn of 1904. Small wonder that he stayed, falling in love not only with Charmian Kittredge, but the golden vineyard countryside, and its plaza-centered pueblo village. Sonoma had been the home of both General Vallejo and Count Agoston Haraszthy. As perhaps one of California's first planned communities, Sonoma grew from a directive issued by Governor Jose Figueroa on June 24th, 1835. The graceful community was established around a central plaza. The man entrusted with carrying out the plans was a handsome young lieutenant, Mariano, Guadalupe Vallejo.

That seven moons rise over the undulating hills of Sonoma is an Indian legend, but it is true that seven flags have flown over Sonoma County, being those of Spain, England, Imperial Russia, the Mexican Empire, Republic of Mexico, the Bear Flag of California, and since 1846, the Stars and Stripes.

Vallejo saw them all. He came as a young ensign, and died at his gracious estate, as an honored General in 1890. The biography of

General Vallejo is the history of California, simultaneously turbulent, romantic, violent and pastoral.

The heart of the story lies in Sonoma, in the Valley of the Moon. A leisurely visit to "Lachryma Montis", the Vallejo home, now a California State Historical Monument, open to the public, is an invitation to the sensitively aware, to touch a California yesterday . . . in the drawing room of the house of seven marble fireplaces . . . in the garden's deep shade from Camphor trees brought from China on sailing vessels that also brought unique varieties of oranges from Southeast Asia, great pomelo trees from Malaya . . . by the graceful fountain fronting "El Delirio" the gothic-gazebo cottage which was a retreat for idle hours of General Vallejo's large family.

A mute silver trophy berry spoon presented to the General as *"Maker of Best Red Wine — 1858"* proclaims to knowing connoisseurs, the gentility of wine-tasting between Vallejo and Haraszthy which persuaded the noble Hungarian to extend his Sonoma vineyards and cut cellar caves into the stone hills at Buena Vista that very year! More than one hundred years later, you can still see the pick marks in the cellar walls, where Chinese coolies excavated three deep caves into the rocky hillside. Wine-making was more than commercial enterprise, it was the hallmark of landed gentry.

As you look at the silk-lined leather case made to hold the epaulets of General Vallejo, you might almost believe the crunching sound on the gravel outside is the General's carriage rolling up the tree-lined drive. Jack London aimed his own tourist's camera at those ghosts, as well you may.

There is high drama of another sort just a few minutes away, at Buena Vista, the vineyard estate of General Vallejo's contemporary, the incredible Hungarian, Count Agoston Haraszthy. As the biography of Vallejo is California history, the astonishing career of Haraszthy is the history of the wine industry in the State. No thumbnail sketch can capsule the vigour of this titled immigrant, who established, not only many vineyards in California, but single-handedly planted, in the Valley of the Moon, the roots on which today's wine industry thrives. He brought them from Europe in a chronicled official mission of State, commissioned by the Governor of California, and Lincoln's Secretary of State, William H. Seward, in 1861. It brought him, ultimately, financial ruin . . . and everlasting fame.

Guests are welcome every day in the cool tunnel tasting rooms of the Count's winery, fronting a running brook, in the shade of the tallest eucalyptus trees in California. Here is the "Haraszthy Heuriger" or "new wine garden", over the bridge and under the trees, where checkered table-cloths are spread in filtered sunlight. Take a book of verses, for there is a loaf of bread, wine, some cheese, and the greatest kind of contentment to be found!

Buena Vista was a weed-covered estate in 1943, when its ownership and restoration came to Frank and Antonia Bartholomew. To the delight of wine connoisseurs everywhere, a true renaissance occurred at Buena Vista. The old vines began to yield their treasures for the cellars. The earth that had sealed some of the tunnels in the great earthquake that rocked San Francisco in 1906, were excavated. Mr. Bartholomew, executive head of United Press International, found, in wine, the same aesthetic challenge that the founder pursued throughout his life. Gold Medals have come from not only California State Fairs, but European competitions, just as plaudits have come from American astronauts, for Buena Vista wines served in banquets at the Waldorf Astoria, in New York, and from Prince Philip, on a recent American visit. Today, the heritage is shared with the prestige firm, Young's Market Company, of Los Angeles, who are carrying on the traditions brought about by Bartholomew's expanded awareness of the wines. The demand has increased. Winemaker Al Brett and enologist André Tehelistcheff have acquired 700 acres of prime vineyard land lying upon the divide of Napa and Sonoma to be planted to varietals . . . Pinot Noir and Cabernet Sauvignon . . . for a yield in the late '70's.

The late Ambassador, J. D. Zellerbach, who set out 16 acres of vines on a high hillside, 700 feet above sea level, on contoured terraces open to the warm westerly rays of the sun . . . 10 acres of Pinot Noir grapes, and 6 acres of Chardonnay . . . founded another Valley of the Moon trust-in-wine. Crowning the vineyard which he named "Hanzell", from a contraction of his surname and his wife's given name, Hannah, he built a winery with direct architectural inspiration from the celebrated Clos de Vougeot of Burgundy, where the same variety of grapes have grown to make centuries of vinous tradition.

The Ambassador pressed his ideal of winemaking with the highest goals, and equipped the premises with gleaming stainless steel and glass-lined holding tanks and Limousine oak casks from Nuits St. George for aging the vintages that would come with each harvest. He lived to taste only the first few vintages, but happily for those that follow today, his successors, Mr. and Mrs. Douglas Day have found the Valley of the Moon to be the place of their heart's content, and "still the vines, their ancient ruby yield!"

12

For the casual visitor to the Valley of the Moon today, there is treasure to take away. It comes as a generous legacy from yesterday's legendary figures . . . Vallejo, Haraszthy, London . . . as you follow the intimate paths of their monuments . . . in their words, their homes, their land. Each found his own "Valley of the Moon" . . . to be, not alone that part of California terrain named by the Indians poetically from an illusion about the moon rising over many ridges, but as their place of peace and contentment.

What was it Jack London said? *"Happiness is the object of existence."* There are photographs showing him at the helm of a sailing vessel, another, half-naked flexing his biceps, yet another as a correspondent covering the Russian-Japanese war, more, in South Pacific paradise isles, but it was of his mountainside of aged vineyard, where he made a lake, and planted forests, in the Valley of the Moon, that he told Charmian . . . "A sweet land, Mate Woman, a sweet land."

SHERRY

*"O for a beaker full of the
warm South . . ."*

JOHN KEATS

*"Wines that heaven knows when,
Had sucked the fire
of some forgotten sun,
And kept it through
a hundred years of gloom."*

ALFRED LORD TENNYSON

THE SUN SELDOM SHINES through the winter roof of England. At its best and brightest, the sky may have a whitish, yellow glow, but the air is sulphurous from the smoke of a million coal-burning hearths. On rainy days, in London, the lumbering lurch of traffic on wet, black cobbles, accentuates the dullness of the atmosphere, pounding a heavy symphony through the winding concourse of grey streets and gloomy buildings. Leafless trees accentuate the barren cold bleakness of the landscape. There is no relief from winter, beyond the promise of a tiny, coal-burning hearth. Bright yellow and orange travel posters offer dream-escapes to Mediterranean isles, impossible for the time-bound student, or pedestrian worker. The advertisement only accentuates the sunless sky of London. Today I can understand John Keats' yearning, and equally the answer he found in Spanish wine, and the reason for more than four hundred years of popularity Sherry has enjoyed among the winter-locked of England. It is an elixir of sunshine!

If Port is the wine of philosophy, Sherry is the wine of memory. Its golden light conjures the magic of recall. One taste transcends time to a particular moment. So eloquent a liquid must make an indelible mark when first encountered by anyone, and from such impression, I was not immune. I remember not only the wine, but the sudden mouthful of sweetness, its warmth, relieving the penetrating cold of a rainy, dark, grey London afternoon, after a long walk beside the Thames, in search of the site of Shakespeare's Globe Theatre.

15

The author of my little volume of "London Walks" had promised to "make the stones of its streets cry out to those who tread them, more history than they have previously known." And indeed, they had. Thirty years later, the same quest might still let me ignore the rain, the cold, wet, sodden shoes with the reward of walking through Shakespeare's London, and finding the markers of his being. Beyond memory, too, a glass of "The Quiet Drink"...a rich East India Oloroso Sherry, to punctuate the re-telling of the walk's discoveries, would still be the most appropriate mark for a late winter afternoon.

In 1587, that Elizabethan favorite, Sir Francis Drake returned from a plundering raid on the port of Cadiz, with 2900 butts of mellow Sherry in the holds of his raiding armada. It was no accidental prize! The taste for the wine was already on the English tongue. Shakespeare was no stranger to the wine, which frequently filled his cup at the Mermaid Tavern. None but a Sherry drinker could write the encomium he shouted from the mouth of Falstaff;

"...A good sherris-sack hath a two-fold operation in it. It ascends me into the brain; dries me there all the foolish and dull and crudy vapours which environ it; makes it apprehensive, quick, forgetive, full of nimble, fiery, and delectable shapes; which, deliver'd o'er to the voice, the tongue, which is the birth, becomes excellent wit. The second property of your excellent sherris is, the warming of the blood; which, before cold and settled, left the liver white and pale, which is the badge of pusillanimity and cowardice; but the sherris warms it and makes it course from the inwards to the parts extreme: it illumineth the face, which as a beacon gives warning to all the rest of this little kingdom, man, to arm; and then the vital commoners and inland petty spirits muster me all to their captain, the heart, who, great and puffed up with this retinue, doth any deed of courage; and this valour comes of sherris.... If I had a thousand sons, the first humane principle I would teach them should be, to forswear thin potations and to addict themselves to sack."

(HENRY IV, PART II, IV. 3.)

The age of Sack began for England in 1517, when a Spanish Duke granted special privileges to English merchants who would ship the wines of his country from Jerez de la Frontera. The word "Sherry" is a corruption of the name of that town, applied to its wine, which was *seco*...sack...dry! Terminology is no less corrupt today, for a wine romantically called "Dry Sack" cannot truly be properly described as being without sweetness, which is "dry."

But the wine of my memory was of a noble sweetness, a rich softness of texture, and a color of smoldering bronze. Only a few days later, in another English drawing room, I tasted another wine called Sherry, but its color was of white gold and the taste curiously compelling. I learned the meaning of "dry", and the English custom of "Sherry and biscuits" which enjoyed almost universal service on a silver tray at five o'clock. This green-olive dry wine had another name, as Spanish as its origin . . . *Amontillado*. How could two wines, both called Sherry, both from Spain be so totally different in character? Such a simple question begins many a wine-lover's odyssey of tasting, a pleasant preoccupation that can last a lifetime, point reason in travel. Wine countries, all over the world, invite the curious tourist to taste the earth of the vineyard. Sharing the enthusiasm which springs from taste agreement is often the beginning of friendship . . . another dividend to be found along the wine trail.

The heartland of Sherry is the province of Andalusia. Architectural echoes of the Moors are everywhere along the way, from Seville, or Gibraltar. On the rolling hills of Jerez de la Frontera, it leaps over time and architecture, and is heard in the plaintive song of a shepherd, five hundred years after the Spanish re-conquest. Ferdinand and Isabella encouraged the wine industry. Vineyards, planted by the Romans, had been neglected by the Moors. But the Queen who pledged her jewels for Columbus' voyage-to-the-Indies, responded to the demand for Sack. Growers extended their vineyards to the white, calcareous hills of Jerez. In England, even the war with Spain did little to diminish the demand, bringing rousing cheers for cargoes captured at sea, to supply the taverns of old Londontown! Falstaff's loving glorification of "sherris-sack" was ernest tribute to the wine that became eternal in its popularity. Prototypes appeared in vineyard lands everywhere to satisfy the taste for "Sherry."

It is an over-simplification to speak of Sherry as "dry" or "sweet". The range of taste, like the notes of a musical scale, touches every note along the way. The music of your choice may be indicated by the time of day, the acompanying food, or the tenor of your mood. The shelves of your wine-merchant or super-market have examples of every category, from Spain, California, and even New York! Pale, dry, brilliant wines rivalling the Martini as an *apéritif*, stand at one end of the scale, which runs all the way to dark and mysteriously sweet, cream sherries of velvet richness.

How is this accomplished?

The answer to the enigma of the taste and types of Sherries began with the intriguing adventures Pasteur found under the lens of his microscope, in the fickle behavior of yeast cells, those microorganisms which accomplish the transformation of grape juice to wine . . . or vinegar. As wild yeasts, they live in the visible, dusty "bloom" on the skin of the grape, where vines have been bearing for many, many years, even centuries. Until comparatively recently, within the last decade, the Spanish "flowering" yeast was thought to be a protozoan, identified as "mycoderma vini", but that same erratic yeast is now identified as merely another member of the *Saccharomyces* family . . . S. *beticus!*

After the Palomino grapes have been trodden by men wearing hob-nailed shoes, and the fermentation subsides from its tumultous seething primary activity, the new wine is syphoned off into oak casks, and filled only partially. In any other wine country but Spain, this would spell disaster, and invite those unwanted vinegar-making yeasts, *Acetobacter.* But here, in that air-space, an invisible population of indigenous aerobic yeasts, a microflora, makes its home on the surface of the wine. By springtime, or before, a tell-tale, creamy white film has covered the surface of the wine. It is called *la flor*, the flowering has marked this new wine as a *fino* sherry. This is that S. *beticus*, flor yeast, which happily thrives on air, alcohol, and acetic acid. Feeding upon the new wine, it brings about curious flavor changes, those tastable nuances which mark the Spanish *amontillado, manzanilla*, and the captivating *apéritif* wine of Córdoba, *montilla*, as bone-dry as a Martini, but of singular charm. But this "flowering" does not occur in all the casks . . . only in some. This capricious whimsy of Señor Beticus, in choosing his vinous abode, nominates those other newly-made Sherries, to the more common category, called *oloroso*, from which the sweeter Sherries will be made. Brandy is added, and a boiled-down concentrate of the sweet juice of the Pedro Ximénès grape. These will be the golden and cream Sherries . . . like Harvey's famous Bristol Cream, or Williams and Humbert's Walnut Brown. The world-famous La Ina of Pedro Domecq is an amontillado . . . pale, dry, golden, flavored by the flowering of capricious yeasts. This is that *Dry Sherry*, born from the soil of the mother-vineyard, as host to *la flor*, which becomes, after master-blending, and solera aging, the wine of nutty, olive-richness so tantalizing to the palate that it can create appetite!

The leading laboratory of the wine world today is in California, at the University of California campus at Davis. In these brief paragraphs, only a fleeting glimpse of adventure can be revealed, within the wine-

18

story. "Where the telescope ends, the microscope begins. Which of the two has the grander view?" Professor Maynard Amerine, of UC-Davis chose this quotation from Victor Hugo to begin his explanation of the microorganisms and wine, in his comprehensive book about "Wine". Our motive here, merely an invitation to explore that tasting country called "Sherry" as it invites you quietly from the labels on the shelves in your daily marketing commerce.

The sunswept vineyard hills of California grow the same *Palomino* and *Pedro Ximénès* vines that green the dazzling chalk-white landscape of Jerez de la Frontera. Our leading vintners have even imported that capricious "flowering" yeast, in the re-creation of intriguing appetizer Sherries. Patient aging, in tiered casks of the *solera* system, further institutes the tradition of Spain in this one-time outpost of empire.

From the abundance of varieties, there is Sherry to drink before, with, and after meals. There is no such thing as "cooking Sherry." As with all wines used in cooking, the alcohol is evanescent, being volatile with the application of heat, nought but the flavor remains. The better the wine, the better the flavor. Cooking wine is the most expensive wine you can afford for that purpose. The dry Sherry you will use to aromatize a sauce for sole, may equally serve as an *apéritif*. A sweet cream Sherry to soak a sponge-cake for Trifle, enriches that English dessert and accounts for its centuries of popularity. It is also the flavor-agent of the humble custard, that in Spanish tradition, is heightened to culinary importance as the versatile *flan*, ornamented with luscious ripe fruit.

From our treasury of favorite recipes, there's little chance of anything but sweet success in the careful preparation of this Andalusian classic:

FLAN DE SEVILLE

In a heavy pan, heat 1 cup of sugar until melted and golden to make caramel. Add 1 tablespoon of water, cook briefly, stirring constantly. Pour this caramel syrup into 12 custard cups, one at a time, tilting to coat sides evenly. Cool.

Prepare a rich custard. Beat 8 eggs lightly. Add 3/4 cup sugar, 1 teaspoon vanilla, 1 tablespoon cream Sherry, and a fleck of salt; stir in 4 cups of scalded milk; blend and pour into caramelized cups: Set cups into a metal pan with 1 inch of hot water. Bake about 30 minutes at 350°, or until a silver knife inserted comes out clean. Unmold onto a platter when warm, allowing space between each custard for a garnish with halves of ripe peaches, or chunks of ripe pineapple Garnish with flourishes of whipped cream piped in elegant ribbons. Serves 12.

SHERRY TRIFLE

It was my great and good fortune to be served a magnificent production of this traditional English sweet, in London, which sent me hunting for it again and again on menus thereafter, only to have a series of miserable disappointments. Trifle can be as miserable or marvelous as its ingredients. That is the main secret of its creation. It is sponge cake, sweet Sherry, preserved or fresh fruit, and custard. That's all the makings. But if any one ingredient is less than perfect, so is the dish!

2 layers of golden sponge cake
1 cup strawberry, raspberry, or
   apricot jam, or . . . even better . . . as
   much crushed, sweetened fresh fruit
1 cup Cream Sherry
   (or Malmsey Madeira)
½ cup Brandy
1 ounce Jamaican Rum
8 egg yolks
¾ cup sugar

4 cups cream, scalded
1 teaspoon vanilla
½ teaspoon almond extract
1 cup heavy cream, whipped,
   sweetened
Blanched almonds, maraschino
   cherries,
   or sliced fresh strawberries,
   lady-fingers, or macaroons

Line a serving dish with one layer of cake. Spread it generously with jam, or crushed fruit. Sprinkle with half of the Sherry. Top with the second layer of cake. Combine remaining Sherry and Brandy and pour over cake. Let it stand until all the wine and Brandy has been absorbed.

In the top of a double-boiler, beat the egg yolks with sugar, until thick. Slowly stir scalded cream. Cook over simmering, not boiling, water, stirring constantly until the custard coats the spoon. Remove from heat, and stir in flavoring extracts. Cool. Pour custard over cake layers. Chill. Flavor whipped cream with Rum. Decorate top of trifle with flourishes of whipped cream through a pastry bag, garnishing with almonds, cherries and/or fresh fruit, lady-fingers, macaroons. Chill thoroughly before serving. Makes 12-16 servings.

The Italian version of this famous dessert is called *Zuppa Inglese*-literally, "English soup" though no one knows exactly why. That it was the result of English tourists in Italy in the days of the romantic poets strains credulity. It is hard to believe their demand for the dessert reminded the Italians of the way they made "soup"! In making it their own, they often cover it totally with meringue, instead of whipped cream, smooth it with a moistened spatula, decorate the top fancifully with candied peel, sprinkle it lightly with superfine sugar, and then put it into a moderate oven, under watchful eyes, until it all becomes a pale ivory. Chilled at room temperature, and then, in the refrigerator.

Cheddar Cheese Dollars

Perfect companions to either Dry Sherry, or Brut Champagne, as an ideal single appetizer, are these short wafers.

½ pound sharp Cheddar cheese
  grated
¼ pound butter
½ teaspoon salt

1¼ cups flour
⅛ teaspoon dry mustard
Few grains, cayenne

Combine grated cheese with butter and all remaining ingredients. Work mixture until smooth. Form into a cylinder the diameter of a silver dollar. Wrap in foil and chill. Slice like refrigerator cookies, ¼ inch thick. Bake in a preheated 350° oven for 10 minutes, or until lightly colored. Cool. Serve.

MADEIRA

...THE BITTERSWEET TASTE OF HISTORY

Connoisseurs are more and more taking notice
of Madeira wines, and their lead is bringing back
to Madeira and Malmsey the large measure of public
interest which those excellent wines so well deserve.

ANDRÉ L. SIMON

IT HAS FOREVER been the tendency of man to belittle his own times, and out of present misery, mistakenly sigh after a more eloquently peaceful past. Truth does not bear out the fiction of this pastime, but the truthful taste of history, lies where Pliny found it, even in antique Rome . . . in wine. *In vino veritas.*

While each and every product of the grape has closely followed the slow march of 5,000 years of civilization, from the glamorous Egyptian dynasties to less ornamental, but technological vinous perfection of the 20th century, the wines of Madeira tie history and taste together, with man's yearnings for Utopia. The search is doomed to frustration, but its legacy are all kinds of monuments, from pyramids to poems, new worlds . . . and new wines, born of those personal yesterdays.

The story of Madeira wine begins in the century following the discovery of that combination of saltpetre, sulphur, and charcoal which had made possible the spectacular displays of fireworks which the Emperor Kubilai Khan had staged for Marco Polo, but which the Western world dubbed for military use as *gunpowder!* It flamed the pages of the 15th century. Portuguese and Spanish ships were the first to mount cannons on their navy brigs. England's Henry V was quick to see how guns might be more than anti-personnel weapons, and commanded construction of the first 1,000 ton men-of-war. This was the time of the prolonged Wars of the Roses, of noble houses against noble houses, as Richard, Duke of Gloucester, made his way with bloody hands to the Throne. The English Channel was a causeway more of war than commerce. Joan of Arc rose in a flash legend with victory over the English at Orleans, in 1429.

23

Before the end of this century, Columbus had sailed for the Indies, in search of the spice islands, on a westerly course. That voyage, and those of Vasco da Gama opened up a New World, colonial rivalries, securing voyages, treaties, revolutions, and competitive trade.

Shakespeare made dramatic use of historical fact in the chronological succession of the English throne through these turbulent times, which indelibly etched the murder of George, Duke of Clarence, by drowning in a butt of Malmsey-wine, in *The Tragedy of Richard the Third*, which tells us not only that Madeira wine was in common trade from the Portuguese dominion in that fatal year, for Clarence, in 1478, but that it had taken only a few brief generations for this new wine to dominate the world of public acceptance in international trade. The first vines ever planted on the island of Madeira, were brought there by Joao Gonçalves Zarco, with the blessing of John the Bastard King of Portugal in 1420.

The hero of our story was a brash young commoner, who claimed the hand of a nobleman's daughter, boldly addressed the King, and for the sheer bravura of his spirit, won not only his lovely Constanca, but companionship to Prince Henry, the Navigator, son of the King, entrusted with patroling the coastal waters against invasion by marauding Moors. After the first of such encounters, Zarco suggested fixing cannons to the main deck of their flagship. The fire-belching sides of Prince Henry's ship terrorized the Moors. The battle at Ceuta on the Gibraltar Straits of North Africa, brought quick victory, and Zarco won a ship for his own command.

In 1418, Zarco daringly pointed the prow of his ship south and west, in the direction of the setting sun, out towards the far edge of the shelf of the sea (for the world was still flat), and 400 miles off the coast of Morocco, he sighted an uncharted island, put in, christened his discovery Porto Santo. It was totally uninhabited. When he returned to Lisbon, he was undismayed to learn that both French and Spanish had been there before him. With the undaunted courage of youth, he promised the King that he would, with only a few ships and provisions, settle the island, and hold it against all comers. A nod of the crown sent Zarco swiftly back to Porto Santa in June of 1419. The tiny island proved too small a prize for the enterprising Zarco. He itched to see what lay further south, where massive clouds constantly billowed above the horizon. On an August morning, he sailed south to satisfy his curiosity. Only hours later, a great green mountain rose out of the sea before him, forested solidly from its 6,000 foot heights to a ravine-ribbed shoreline. He named it Madeira, the wooded island. Here was enough land to challenge a man's ambition, a small island empire to build as a goal of life.

With samples of soil, and dreams of harvests-to-come, Zarco sailed back to Lisbon, captured the approval of his sovereign, gained the title, Captain of Madeira, and the means to secure and develop his dream. With his wife, and a retinue of farmers, seeds, trees, and vines, he returned to Madeira in May of 1420, dropping anchor in a generous inlet. He named it Funchal because of the great profusion of wild fennel growing everywhere. Impenetrable dense forests presented farming problems. Some might question his first command as Governor, but history is grateful. He had cut enough timber for housing; he needed fields for planting vines and sugar-cane. With the boldest resolution, he put fire to the forests. All records indicate that the island burned for seven years. The soil, already enriched with centuries of accumulated, decomposed leaf-mould, now, as he foresaw, was improved by the addition of ash potash. He had made the volcanic, pumice-stone soil, the richest vineyard site in the world. He had also rid the island of all insect pests, mosquitoes, and snakes, even altered the humidity and scale of rainfall. A Venetian visitor, voyaging from Africa in 1455, wrote with true amazement, of Zarco's vineyard. The *Malvasia* vines, which had been imported from Crete, produced more grapes than leaves! The vines were trained on trellised poles, and from a sloping lattice-work, allowed the *vendangeurs* to reach up for the heavy clusters, instead of bending over in the back-breaking traditions of the mainland. The visitor also observed that enough wine was made for the export of numerous 126-gallon pipes. The demand grew throughout Zarco's lifetime, extending the areas of planting even onto some of the high slopes and plateaux. But it was the wine from the lower vineyards, of ample sunshine and warmth, of sugar-rich grapes, that brought Madeira its first reputation. This wine, called Malmsey by the English, in which the unfortunate Duke of Clarence was drowned, is still in greatest demand. It remains, like the Paradise-island itself, Zarco's monument.

In the centuries that followed, three other principal grape species were planted... *Sercial* from the banks of the Rhine, *Boal* (*Bual* in Portuguese), and *Verdelho*, which, with the *Malvasia*, or Malmsey, produce a range of taste from dry to sweet, and all with a bittersweet pungency and soil-echoing recall in aroma. This taste characteristic, drawn from the soil by the tendrils of the vine, bows, for the knowing, to Zarco's forest fire.

In the 17th century, when Charles II, England's resplendent Restoration monarch, took Catherine of Braganza of Portugal as his wife, he was offered the island of Madeira as a part of her dowry. He chose to take Tangier instead, but he did not refuse the wines of the island. A decree of 1663, prompted without doubt by English merchants who foresaw rival demands upon the limited supplies of Malmsey wine, made the products of Madeira the exclusive barter of English ships bound for "Lands, Islands, Plantations, Colonies, Territories, or Places to His Majesty belonging in Asia, Africa or America." Pipes, barrels, hogshead casks of Madeira became common cargo to the American colonies. From this practice, a most remarkable improvement in the wine was noticed. Stored below-decks, the wines were in constant rocking motion. The ships invariably put in to sweltering, tropical ports of the West Indies. When the casks of wine arrived in the colonies of Virginia, the rough young wines had become miraculously mellow! Far from being damaged by the exceptional heat, the "voyage to the Indies" had brought about a transformation in taste.

The Malmsey-Madeira of Zarco's time, and even of Shakespeare's day, was a heady red wine. But with the Portuguese alliance, English palates became accustomed to the wines of Opporto which were fortified with grape brandy. The practice was adopted in Madeira, but in their own unique style. Brandy was introduced at three stages of winemaking. First, into the troughs where the grapes were crushed, then into the *mosto*, and finally into the finished wine, in quantities calculated only to slow, but not stop the fermentation. Grapes harvested in the mountain vineyards, too far away from the wineries at Funchal, were thrown into the *lagares*, stone troughs just wide enough for six men abreast, to trample the vintage barefooted. The *mosto* would then be transported in goatskins, down the mountain trails on the backs of the vineyard workers, to Funchal, where fermentation would bring the wine to its primary finish as *vinho claro*. Next, into a hot chamber, *estufa*, before being fortified with brandy for the fullness of *vinho generoso*. The rocking voyages on ships, through tropical heat, was bound to set off final fermentation. The natural abundance of grape-sugar in the wine, with limited amounts of brandy, not only brought added strength to the wine, but finished off the life of any remaining yeasts. Today, the *estufa* substitutes for the "voyage to the Indies." Long aging in wood is still given to all the wines of Madeira, and they still can claim unlimited age as an ally. Among all the wines of the world, Madeira alone benefits unceasingly with age . . . in each variety.

Those variations, caused, among the leading citizens of the American colonies, the Gentleman's preoccupation . . . with wine-tasting. George

Washington, John Adams, John Hancock, Mad Anthony Wayne, and Peter Stuyvesant all boasted pride collections of Madeira wines, and met at Madeira parties to weigh solemnly the merits of Malmsey, Sercial, and Verdelho from different ships and shippers. They compared costs, color, taste, and methods of storage. They did not believe in bottling. Kegs or demi-johns were the only acceptable containers to give the wine legroom for growing. The fate of a prized Madeira was as exciting as Washington's victory at Trenton, or at least, so it is put down in the little book shown in our accompanying illustration, published at the turn of the century, by one S. Weir Mitchell, whose antecedents could recall those times directly. He quotes a letter from a Revolutionary War Colonel, Lambert Cadwalader, to an aid at Lancaster, in 1776: *"Take particular care of the red chest clampt with iron herewith sent, which contains some bonds and mortgages which I could not take out, the key being lost; and also that you would be kind enough to let the two quarter-casks of Madeira, painted green, be deposited in some safe place under lock and key in your cellar, if possible where you keep your own liquors in a safe place, as I value them more than silver and gold in these times of misfortune and distress."* Could any wine have more sincere testimonial?

Why, you may well ask, did such wines fall from favor and popular use? The island of Madeira was struck, in 1852, with a ravaging plant fungus, *oidium*, peculiar to humid climate. It wiped out almost all the vineyards of the island. A second blow came with the more familiar, but equally deadly root louse infection, *phylloxera*, only a few years later. The disaster could have meant the end of Madeira wines, for the farmers could not sustain the loss. Their shippers came to their aid. The old firms, Leacock, Cossart, and Gordon, with others, gave financial assistance and reason to replant, on hardy, disease-resistant American rootstock. But supplies of wines had been severely curtailed. Prohibition, the blight that hit America, ended the gentle custom of Madeira service which had been nurtured by our initial aristocracy of statesmen. "A Madeira Party" was not in the tempo of the times. Today, in seemingly unequalled and generally depressed national spirits, Madeira is re-emerging because of its mood-inducing comfort, as a curio worthy of the attention of the wine cognoscenti. Without too much difficulty, you can find vintage Madeiras from the last century. These *vinhos generosos* all have known patient aging in wood. Some are products of a *solera* system, whose dominating character stems from wines that were young a century ago.

Always in the vanguard of public taste, the Paul Masson Vineyards of northern California, with a well-aged stock of wines from true varieties of dessert-wine grapes, blended a California Madeira, which, at a recent blindfold tasting, matched the most mellow examples imported from the wooded isle of Zarco. It has become an indispensable item in my own cellar for both kitchen and bar. You'll find it modest in price, extravagant in virtues.

Madeira today is always a pleasant surprise to guests . . . a special compliment, no matter if you choose the dry *Sercial*, which is a more opulent aperitif than Sherry, — the middle course of *Verdelho*, or the dessert-rich *Boal*, or *Malmsey*. The freshness of finish, clean bitter-sweet after-taste in the mouth, suggests that a decanter in an executive office could argue its service as a replacement-in-style for the eleven o'clock coffee-and-cigarette break. Even wine ritualists allow cigarettes with Madeira. The double-lipped 18th century crystal "solitaire" in our photograph, filled with water, was invented for rinsing the bowl of a single wineglass for a second tasting. With traditional silver and crystal, Madeira lends itself to style. As an accompanying snack, the simplicity of these bland English-style biscuits, adapted from a recipe by Elizabeth Craig, are clearly marked for the elevenish Madeira . . . in the executive suite.

SHREWSBURY SNIPPETS

½ cup butter	2 cups flour, sifted before measuring
4 tablespoons sugar	½ teaspoon baking powder
1 egg	Grated rind of 1 lemon

Cream butter and sugar. Beat in egg, then flour, sifted with baking powder. Add lemon rind. Mix well. Turn out onto floured board. Knead until smooth. Roll out to ¼ inch thickness. Cut into fanciful shapes . . . daisies, diamonds, oblong wafers. Place on floured cookie sheet. Bake in pre-heated 375° oven for 5 minutes or so, until they are pale, pale gold. Cool on cake rack. Store in tight container. Serve with Madeira.

MADEIRA FLIP

Raymond Oliver, the erudite Proprietor of the great Paris restaurant *Le Grand Véfour*, nominates, in the category of aphrodisiacs, or love potions, the Flip. The most inspirational of such is surely made with rich, old and mellow Malmsey Madeira. To make one serving would be unthinkable; our recipe is for two!

2 whole eggs	Fresh grated nutmeg
2 teaspoons superfine sugar	(ready-grated is impossible,
6 ounces Malmsey Madeira	totally lacking in fresh aroma)
1 ounce brandy	2 elegant stemmed wine goblets
4 or 5 ice cubes	

Combine all the liquid ingredients, with the ice cubes, in a mixing glass. Cover it with a shaker, and grasping them firmly with both hands, shake vigorously. Remove the shaker, place a strainer over the mixing glass, and pour out into the generous-sized wine goblets. Sprinkle the top with nutmeg.

As Monsieur Oliver quite rightly says: "One man's aphrodisiac can be another man's disappointment." The heart of the matter really lives only in the minds of the protagonists. The first postulate before the Flip is assembled, and shaken, is that it is after all, only a prelude to pleasure. *That*, after all, is the symphony.

Into this same category of inspirational foodstuffs, must certainly go this Lucullan recipe for presenting jumbo fresh strawberries... when they are at their most fragrant peak of perfection. It is a treasured recipe of the famous Blue Fox Restaurant in San Francisco, and given to me by Mario Mondin and Piero Fassio who have, in two decades, brought this one-time small French restaurant into the world of great American dining rooms. This recipe, made with loving hands at home, can only be a tribute to those to whom it is served. A love potion? Certainly!

STRAWBERRIES A LA BLUE FOX

Jumbo strawberries	2 tablespoons Marsala, Madeira,
2 egg yolks	Port, or Sherry
2 tablespoons granulated sugar	¼ cup confectioners' sugar
	1 cup heavy cream

1. Wash strawberries in cold water; drain well; hull. From point, slit each berry into quarters, *but don't cut thru' bottom*. Refrigerate.
2. Make Sabayon Cream: In top of double-boiler with portable electric mixer at medium speed, beat yolks with granulated sugar & Sherry until well combined.
3. Place over boiling water; beat at medium speed until mixture is thick and forms soft peaks when beater is lifted (about 5 minutes). Remove from heat.
4. Immediately set top of double-boiler in bowl of ice; continue beating until mixture is cool — about 2 minutes. Let stand in ice in refrigerator 30 minutes longer.
Meanwhile:
5. In medium bowl, combine ¼ cup powdered sugar and the heavy cream (1 cup). Refrigerate along with beater for 30 minutes.
6. Add chilled cooked mixture to chilled cream mixture; beat until stiff.
7. Fill each strawberry with Sabayon mixture using pastry bag with decorating tip, bringing Sabayon mixture to a peak at top. Refrigerate.
8. To serve: Sprinkle lightly, filled berries with confectioners' sugar. Arrange on mound of crushed ice. Makes 8-10 servings.

VERMOUTH

AND OTHER APÉRITIF WINES

THE GENESIS of Vermouth salutes Hippocrates, the father of modern medicine. That ancient worthy learned the secret of extracting the essence of bitter herbs which had the power to awaken lost appetite, by dissolving them in wine-alcohol, then making the steeped brew more palatable by the addition of honey. All kinds of aromatic wines were known to both the Greeks and Romans, who added everything from pine resin and poppy, to seawater, almonds and smoke, but it was not until 1786 that one formula captured universal favor. It was the secret of Antonio Carpano, of Turino, who, at the Piazza Castello combined a hauntingly exotic collection of balms as redolent of mystery as an Oriental bazaar. He called it *Liquoreria Merendazo*. The base wine was Moscato d'Asti, strengthened with pure brandy, sweetened with sugar, and infused with a steeped wine-brew of bark, seeds, herbs, spices, petals, and leaves, and most definitively, the yellow-bead blossoms of a forest shrub, botanically named for the goddess of the hunt, Artemis, *Artemisia absinthium*, commonly known as *wormwood* . . . in German, *Wermut*.

Wormwood . . . Absinthe . . . Pernod! This triptych of terror, not totally unrelated to vermouth, persists in mystery, an awesome nepenthe, insidious, even lethal. Dégas immortalized the pathos of addiction in an unforgettable canvas of hooked dejection called "The Absinthe Drinkers." The opalescent liqueur, invented in Couvet, Switzerland near the end of the 18th century by an exiled Frenchman, Dr. Ordinaire, owed some, but not all of its insistent appeal to the leaves, not the flowers, of wormwood. The toxic leaves, allegedly damaging to the nervous system, were a masquerade for, among other aromatics, a beverage that was 136° proof! The "Green Muse" as it was known to Parisian bistro habituées, could quite well have been responsible for many crimes, and even insanity, merely from its potent alcoholic strength. The recipe was sold, in 1797, to Henri-Louis Pernod, whose name on the label became synonymous with the product. Before World War I, its sale was prohibited in both France and Switzerland, when the Pernod firm moved to Tarragona, Spain. Absinthe is still banned

31

in most countries of the western world for the dubious attributes of wormwood leaves, but the yellow-green, anise-flavored liqueur enjoys unlimited café popularity in Spain. In our 20th century world of newer hallucenogenics, absinthe is probably a harmless pretender. The licorice-tasting Pernod at your local bar, made in France, or Spain, follows Dr. Ordinaire's original formula, but is minus the noxious wormwood leaves.

The fate of Signor Carpano's aromatic experiment with wine and wormwood blossoms in Turino, has no tinge of tragedy. It was the beginning of a whole new and expanding saga for the wine world, and the winelover. Other wineries copied Signor Carpano's stimulating *apéritif*, with their own variations. Turin became the center of the vermouth world. Carpano is still one of the leading producers, but who has not heard of Cinzano, Campari, Martini & Rossi, and Ruffino? The vermouth of Italy accounts for almost one-fourth of the country's wine production, 600,000 hectolitres with a value of 15 thousand million lire!

How is it made? It is easy to describe, but a delicate and complex thing to do. It begins today, as it began with Signor Carpano, with a sound basic wine, if white, probably a fragrant muscat, and if red, one of the straightforward wines of Piedmont, or even from Calabria or the island of Sicily. The base wine then receives sufficient grape brandy to bring its strength up to about 18 per cent alcohol. For a sweet vermouth, a *mistelle*, unfermented grape juice, stabilized with brandy, is added. If a darkening of color is required, this is accomplished with both age, and the addition of caramel. Next comes the infusion of those choice herbs, barks, seeds, and spices, the aromatic agents. Even in the 18th century, when the art of vermouth was only beginning to be known, cargoes of spices came to the harbors of Venice, Genoa, and Pisa from the Orient . . . cardamon, cloves, ginger, sandalwood, nutmeg, anise, coriander, cinnamon, hyssop, bitter-orange, rose leaves from Bengal, Peruvian quinine bark, sage, marjoram, angelica, camomile, gentian, elder flowers, and of course, wormwood blossoms. You are always welcome to visit the great houses of Turin Vermouth today, but you will always discover the doors are closed where the select infusion is blended. Each house carefully guards the secret of its own formula.

The basic wine is left in contact with the infusion, agitated with wooden paddles in great blending vats, which are sometimes heated. Then, like steeped tea, it is drawn off, pasteurized, refrigerated to remove any precipitation, and filtered. After a prolonged rest, it may be bottled and shipped.

French vermouth, in the beginning, followed its own pattern of taste preference. It was dry, and white. The vast output of undistinguished white wines of the Midi became a logical source for the production of *apéritif* wines, transformed with aromatics to a new importance. The French taste, which cut the sweetness down to almost zero, emphasized the magic of the wormwood blossoms, adding only a few herbs, spices, and peels. The British discovered that French vermouth made a very jolly combination with gin, which lead quite naturally to the Dry Martini . . . "Gin and French." New Yorkers found the sweet Italian Vermouth harmonized with Bourbon, and the Manhattan cocktail was born.

The early tradition differences still persist, and many a call will come simply for "French" or "Italian" resulting in some confusion, for in both countries now, under proprietory labels, one winery is apt to produce both sweet and dry types. *French* and *Italian* are no longer synonyms for *dry* and *sweet;* nationality should only be used to specify the origin of the vermouth, and not its type. Today, American vermouth sales far exceed those of any foreign label in this market.

The demand for pale, almost colorless Martinis, clear, ice-cold, and non-fragrant, nominated dry vermouth to the edge of extinction. But from the same action, came a reaction, double-edged. As an answer to the call for a silvery, pale vermouth, one evolved, of rare delicacy, in Chambery, in the Savoie, scented exquisitely of sun-dried herbs, non-insistent, and delightful in itself. It improved the taste, heightened the appeal of that "instant insanity", the vermouthless Martini. It pointed the way, as well, to vermouth, as an *apéritif* remedy for the post-luncheon haze of the high-proof cocktail.

A few months ago, *Time Magazine,* under the caption of *What's In* for the *Modern Living* department, noted that "lighter-spirited European drinks as Lillet Orange (Lillet vermouth, soda, a slice of orange), the Americano (Campari, Cinzano dry vermouth, soda) or just plain Campari and soda" were becoming prominent contenders at the bars of the nation's in-spots. Vermouth-Cassis, which once held sway among the literati of the Parisian left bank, is again fashionable in top-flight restaurants. All of the patent formula wines . . . Dubonnet, both red and blonde, St. Raphael, and Byrrh . . . indelibly French, have become fashionable alternates to palate-searing cocktails. Like classic vermouth, they begin with a good base wine, and depart along time-

33

hallowed sorcery, that herb and flower-petal steeping, quite worthy of sensing. It is equally delightful to discover how good Noilly Prat is with just a twist of lemon, over ice . . . or Chambery Dolin, or Boissiere. If the "Perfect Manhattan" is made with half sweet and half dry vermouth, plus Bourbon, why not try a "Perfect Vermouth" . . . simply half and half of each, dry and sweet, over ice, with a twist of lemon? Premium vintners, Almadén, and Paul Masson both produce excellent sweet and dry vermouths. The renaissance of vermouth has also brought a potent cocktail in its wake, from Europe . . . the Negroni, one-third sweet vermouth, one-third gin, one-third Campari bitters, ice, and soda.

Last, and far from least, is the newly recognized value of vermouth . . . for the kitchen. Why not? All those herbs and spices, incomparably blended, can do wonders, wherever you would use a white wine, or a red wine for cooking, as a marinade, or to bring a special zing to a sauce. Splash some dry vermouth into the court bouillon when you're poaching salmon. Add some to mayonnaise. The Ancient Mariner, a popular steak house at Newport, keeps a bottle of dry vermouth on the pick-up counter; every steak is baptized just before it's served. Hans Prager, the dynamic and highly talented Executive Chef of the world of Lawry's restaurants, explains the secret of one of his favorite dishes . . .

Mushrooms and Vermouth Skillet: Saute button mushrooms (fresh or canned. If fresh, wipe clean, cut off stems close to the cap) in butter in a small, heavy skillet, preferably enamelled. Add salt and pepper, a tablespoon of lemon juice. Shake them about a bit. At the last minute, just before serving, add 1 jigger of dry vermouth, 1 pat of butter, 1 tablespoon of chopped parsely, and a sprinkling of coarse-ground (Kosher) salt.

For a very special occasion, you might wish to try this vermouth-inspired treatment of lamb. It is astonishingly simple, and simply elegant! The sauce is tricky, but possible!

Gigot Persillade au Vermouth

Ask the butcher to skin a leg of lamb for you. Marinate it for 12 hours with a sliced lemon, several sprigs of fresh rosemary, and parsley, and 12 crushed whole peppercorns and 3 cups of dry vermouth. Turn it every now and then, and keep it covered with foil. Pour a 10 pound sack of rock salt into a collander. Pour water over it and allow it to drain thoroughly. Place a ¼-inch bed of salt in the bottom of a casserole which will accommodate the leg of lamb. Remove the lamb from the marinade. Make deep incisions with a sharp knife, and stuff the slits with parsley. Place the lamb, fat side up, on the salt, and pour the remaining salt around and completely over it. Insert a meat thermometer into the roast. Place the casserole in a 300° oven until the thermometer registers 175°-180°. The time will depend upon the size of the roast. The salt will form a solid crust and lift off easily. The lamb will be juicy, brown, and delectable!

LEMON-CAPER SAUCE

In the top of a double boiler, combine 3 egg yolks, 1 tablespoon of lemon juice, 1 teaspoon arrowroot, 1 teaspoon salt, and a few grains of cayenne. Whisk all of this together with a wire beater, gently, over hot, but not boiling water, slowly adding, stirring constantly, ¾ cup of warm chicken stock. When the sauce is thick enough to coat the back of a spoon, set it aside, off the fire, still over the hot water, until time to serve. Just before serving, stir into it 3 tablespoons of drained capers, and 1 tablespoon of finely minced parsley.

In almost any place where you would use White Wine, Dry Vermouth brings the added dividend of all those herbs. With Chicken, it's a natural!

CHICKEN VERMOUTH

3-3½ pound frying chicken, disjointed	1 cup seedless grapes, halved
3 tablespoons flour	¾ cup walnut halves
Salt, pepper, ac'cent	½ pound mushrooms, sliced
¼ pound butter or margarine	¼ cup Dry Vermouth

Combine flour, salt, pepper, and accent in a paper bag. Coat pieces of chicken by shaking in paper bag until thoroughly dusted. Saute in butter or margarine until golden brown.

Remove pieces of chicken to a casserole, cover and keep warm.

Saute mushrooms briefly. If necessary, add a little more butter. Remove mushrooms to casserole with chicken.

Deglaze the sauté pan with the Vermouth, over very low heat, releasing all the bits into a rich liquor.

Sprinkle the grapes and walnuts over the top of the chicken and mushrooms. Pour over it, the remaining liquid from the sauté pan. Cover, and place in 300° oven for 30 minutes. Serve with rice.

CHAMPAGNE

ROMAN SOLDIERS, in the days of Julius Caesar, fought and drilled in the low, rolling, wooded hills of France east of Picardy and the Isle de France. The immense plains of open field, *campus*, near Rheims, became *campania* to the Latin generals, *champaign* to the French, the vine-stubbled land, in later years, emerging as the beloved antique province of *Champagne!*

More than the seat of kings, *La Champagne* produced a wealth of wine in the fields of its ecclesiastical duchies. In 1668, Dom Pérignon was appointed to the post of Cellarer of the Benedictine Abbey of Hautvillers, near Epernay. Wines of the Province of Champagne, with centuries of fame from the celebrated fairs which drew merchants from all parts of civilized Europe to this region of the Marne, constituted the principal fiscal revenue of the Abbey. Supervision of the vineyard domain required prodigious vitality. The job of being Cellarer is not, even today, the roly-poly indulgent friar quaffing tankards in a cellar as has been painted through the centuries by romantic artists! Young Dom Pérignon labored in the vineyard fields surrounding the Abbey as both winemaker and vintner, collecting tithes as well, in wine or grapes for the support of the religious order, for the care of the poor and the sick. Wine of the Abbey was its support; religious orders in pre-Revolutionary France had no grants from the State.

Dom Pérignon came to know each vineyard of the area. Wines from a hillside slope might yield less quantity, but concentrate a fragrance lacking in the abundant harvest of a valley reach. As successive years rolled by, and the horse-drawn, two-wheeled carts would bring harvests from the fields of the Abbey cellars for crushing, the intense young friar was determined to make better wine than had existed previously. The archives of the Abbey have documentary evidence that he suggested: "You must marry the wine of this vineyard with that of such another." So was born the blending idea known as *cuvée*, or *tubful!*

The natural miracle known to us as *fermentation*, is the transformation of the sugar-sweetness of ripe grapes, into alcohol through the agency of yeasts which exist as the powdery bloom on the skin of grapes in cluster on the vine. This microscopic dust of natural yeast cells, when crushed into the running juice of the grapes, splits the atoms of natural sugar, in a reproductive process of yeast cells, but only under certain conditions. Cold paralyses, but without killing, wine yeasts. In those less scientific days of Dom Pérignon, it was quite possible that *les vents sauvages de Novembre*, those cold wet and chilling winds of November, turned the stone-walled wine-cellar of the Abbey into a colossal refrigerator, arresting the fermentation of new wines, while yet some grape-sugar remained, unconverted. Not until the warmth of spring, would the yeasts revive, and begin again their reproductive labors of transforming grape juice into wine.

The by-product of fermentation is carbon dioxide, or carbonic acid gas. Imprisoned, in fermenting hops, it becomes the bubbles in beer, and in wine, the sparkle of Champagne!

Even before the day of Dom Pérignon, the wine of the Province of Champagne was noted for its *petillant* effervescence. Here is where the legend of Dom Pérignon's invention of the wine known as *Champagne* is slightly at variance with true fact. He merely set up conditions, in an effort to improve his wines, which allowed the course of nature to concentrate the bubbles in the wine. Local custom had always stoppered wine with a wad of hemp dipped in oil. To make certain that no dust or foreign material might get to his wines, Dom Pérignon stoppered his wines with cork, securing each with a strong tie about the neck of the bottle. When spring came 'round, and the new wine reawakened, the carbon dioxide incidental to this further fermentation could not escape; it remained in the wine. Months later, sampling his wine, the familiar story tells us that once the cork flew from the bottle to the amazement of Dom Pérignon, he tasted the foaming wine and declared: "I am drinking stars!"

Today, there are more than 25,000 acres producing Champagne in the antique province of *La Champagne*. Though the French passionately declare that no other sparkling wine is entitled to the revered name of their terrain, the word has become, through centuries of usage, a generic term. Present regulations of our own Government stipulate only that the place of origin must be in nominal association and direct conjunction . . . and so we have, and will doubtless always have, our own *"California Champagne"*. Centuries have taken the accident out of the sparkle, techniques have been developed to control both quality and quantity of production, but as with any and all wine, it must forever begin with grapes, and they are as many and varied as the ways of a man with a maid! Just so will there be as many different wines, with or without bubbles.

Knowledge unlocks the doors of mystery. Taste is something of a riddle in itself. To discover which, among the hundreds, almost thousands of wines labelled *Champagne*, is the one for you, is the merry adventure of the wine-quest. It begins with the recognition of the abundant variety of taste-sensations presented by the hosts of creative agriculturalists devoted to wine-making. Comparative analysis may rob you of some instant pleasure, but establish markers in memory along your road to discovering better wines. Fundamentally, all wines are good. The pleasure of wine is in finding, and sharing those you believe contain the joyous answer to your thirst. The Champagne Master's success in this commercial world of ours, depends upon his judgement of your taste . . . and your pocketbook! His secrets lie in his choice of wines which make up his *cuvée;* his method of putting the "stars" into the wine involves only the dynamic economics of production method and those inherent costs. Until recently, with the development of the Charmat Bulk Process, there was no such thing as an "inexpensive Champagne." The history of the Champagne trade is an unparalleled drama of elegance, dominated by the most dashing figures of each era and continent. The Nineties would not have been as Gay without the splash of Champagne. Almost thirty million bottles of bubbly per year made those decades golden for French Champagne houses! Theirs was the wine of Grand Dukes in Russia, the Magyars of Hungary, Kaiser Wilhelm of Germany, and across the Atlantic, to Delmonico's, Rector's, and the table of Diamond Jim Brady! Anecdotes of merchant-prince agent-salesmen for Mumm's, Moët, Heidsieck, Clicquot dim twentieth century press-agent promotion stunts. One party at the Savoy, according to André Simon, flooded the gardens and set up a little Venice complete with imported gondolas and gondoliers, all for Moët Champagne and its drive to capture the American market! In far away California, not to be outdone, a young and dynamic Champagne-maker, Paul Masson, made headlines around the world, when his guest, the reigning beauty Anna Held, bathed in Champagne at his vineyard estate! Paul Masson California Champagne is still world-famous, but the zinc-lined tub today belongs to their good rival company of winemakers at Almadén, Paul Masson's original property. Today, both of these illustrious Champagne houses have developed vast new vineyards in San Benito and Monterey Counties as answer to the overwhelming growth of the post-war population explosion around the Bay Area, which consumed vineyards in the overwhelming onrush of housing developments. Fully aware that good wine begins with good grapes, they established prodigously vast vineyard acreage, which will insure California of great wines in the coming decades.

The Champagne process, as briefly as possible, begins with the

Champagne Master's cuvee of white wine. This is, in vintage Champagne, the wine of one year, blended from the wine of such grapes as Pinot Blanc, Pinot Noir, and Pinot Chardonnay. In California, where our years benefit from an uncommonly uniform climate for the ripening of grapes, vintage-dating is of minor consideration to the consumer; all years are good. Should we have a long, hot summer, the Paicines Vineyard of Almadén is equipped with a million dollar agricultural air conditioning system involving 5,000,000 feet of pipe, in an underground system drawn from deep wells, which can sprinkle the entire 4,000 acre vineyard, controlling the humidity and temperature so important to the production of high quality varietal grapes.

Taking a page from the traditions established three hundred years ago by Dom Pérignon, today's Champagne Master is guided only by his creative ability to make a better wine. He may know one of his wines to possess certain qualities of bouquet, and another an uncommon sprightliness in taste. As an artist blends color pigments knowledgably, so the Champagne Master creates his own *Cuvée*. His recipe, if you will, is his own and on it rests the reputation and fame of the house. This still wine, aged a minimum of two years in wood, is then given an addition of "tirage liqueur" of grape sugar and pure wine yeast cultures, to start the secondary fermentation as the wine is bottled and stored horizontally, in great stacks. Fermentation takes place in the bottle, developing as much as 140 pounds of pressure behind crimped cap closure.

As the bubbles develop in the bottle, so does a natural sediment. Getting rid of that sediment . . . makes Champagne an expensive wine! In the classic French method, every bottle is placed neck down in a "riddling rack" where it is turned clockwise, shaken, and jiggled over a period of two years, at least two hundred and fifty times, by hand! Finally, when all of the sediment "claw" and "mask" is captured in the neck of the bottle, it is frozen, and from the enormous pressure behind it, expelled in a disgorging procedure, in which some of the precious wine, too, may escape. American inventiveness was responsible for the development of a complicated device, known as a "transfer star" in which the horizontally stored wines, after completing their secondary fermentation, could be emptied, under pressure, into a large stainless steel tank. Here, in a decanting process, the sediment falling to the bottom, would allow the wine to be drawn off at the top, through a Seitz filter, and into a second holding tank, where it would receive its highly important "dosage" . . . before going to market in its traditional bottle and cap.

Challenge a man's taste . . . be prepared to fight! In days of old, the French liked their Champagne sweet, the Russians, even sweeter! To the French, it was a dessert wine, but who could deny an Englishman his Port with dessert? Champagne? Never! With fish, yes! So the English market developed a dry Champagne in the 19th century which the French called *"brut"*, meaning *"crude"* and *"raw"*. The battle raged past the turn of the century, but as twenty of the thirty million bottles sold went to the English market, Champagne became a dry wine, and its descriptive terminology had to invent degrees of dryness, corresponding to the amount of sweetness in its final "dosage" of Cognac and dissolved rock sugar crystals! From the *Doux* of almost 10% sweetness, seldom, if ever found on the American market, to *Brut* and *Natur* from zero to a fraction of one percent sweetness, you may find a range of dryness . . . *Demi-Sec, Sec, Extra Dry, Brut,* and *Natur,* to suit your own taste, or use in menu-planning.

Sophisticated palates alledgedly prefer the driest wines. Bah, and humbug! Truly sophisticated palates appreciate both sweet and dry wines, but each in its proper place. A dry Champagne is as out of place with dessert as a bikini at a funeral! But as a thirst-quencher on a hot summer afternoon, it is unsurpassed. For the host or hostess, who knows how to entertain wisely, well, and with invisible economy, Champagne flows instead of cocktails. You don't need to wait for a ship-launching, a birthday, anniversary, or a holiday feast to uncork the pleasures of Champagne! Its foaming swirls evoke a spirit of revelry, without the madness of Martinis, with a sense of well-being and luxury no whisky can match.

Which Champagne? Measure the moment first. How much is it worth? What time of day? What mood? What menu? There's a Champagne-answer to each. Maybe its one of the several Charmat Bulk Process, less expensive Champagnes . . . each Cuvée undergoing its secondary fermentation in gauged stainless steel tanks, uniformly given its dosage, and then bottled. The vivacious, capable, intelligently energetic Brother Timothy of Christian Brothers of the Napa Valley, presides over this 20th century abbey with the same original drive that moved Dom Pérignon, seeking only to produce a fine wine for the support of his Order. "Riddling is for the birds!" he once told me, referring to the laborious, time-consuming classic Champagne method. Brother Tim produces one of the best sparkling wines made with the Charmat bulk process. Others utilizing this 20th century method include Lejon, Eden Roc, and Llords & Elwood.

California produces many fine Champagnes today in the classic

"*Methode Champenoise*", with riddling-racks leading to disgorging and refilling the same bottles in which the wine was fermented. Other premium Champagne houses in California avail themselves of the "quality control" principle inherent in the "transfer star" method. Both of these systems still are called "bottle-fermented Champagne." Their added value comes with the time, as much as two years or more, in which the secondary fermentation works within its small prison of glass, and the wine ages to something finer. Almadén, Beaulieu, Korbel, and Paul Masson make Champagne in this premium style, and are the prestige front-runners of California.

As distinctive apéritif Champagne, for undaunted comparison with the finest of France, we nominate Almadén's Blanc de Blancs vintage Cuvée, made entirely from Pinot Chardonnay. The packaging style of Korbel natural bows to the Dom Pérignon bottling of Moët & Chandon, but the wine looks it straight in the eye! The Paul Masson Oeil de Perdrix Pink Champagne is as full of lavish charm as a painting by Renoir! That gentle newcomer, Schramsberg Cuvée de Gamay, delicate salmon in color sends the mind like quicksilver, to a ribbon of rippling satin! In his ivory-tower vineyard, Martin Ray also produces Champagne of Chardonnay fine enough to turn a Gallic nose green with envy and jealous fear. There are other good names, too . . . on Champagne labels of California . . . Heitz, Kornell, Buena Vista, and Weibel. Taste and price will vary, but so does each purse and palate. You may drink it from a slipper, a bath-tub, a jelly-glass, or an elegant crystal flute, but whatever you do, don't disgrace yourself and the wine by destroying its stars with a swizzle stick, that posh platinum or gold item of the jet-set's psuedo-sophistication, which has, as its only effete purpose, whisking the bubbles from the wine. If you're allergic to sparkling wines, leave Champagne alone. And happily if you are among the general, Champagne, the toasting wine, from the moment of its popping-cork salute . . . signals time to remember!

And here's a dessert for a Champagne occasion!

RHUBARB ROSÉ SOUFFLÉ

1 pound rhubarb	Pinch of salt
3 tablespoons water	Rind of 1 orange, grated
4 tablespoons sugar	Whipped Cream
3 egg whites (½ cup)	

Wash the rhubarb. Cut it into 1-inch lengths. Cook briefly over very low heat with the water. When it has softened, stir in the sugar. Cool. Pour into a strainer, allowing the liquid to drain off. Save it. Then add the grated rind of an orange, and whisk all together.

Beat the egg whites to soft peaks, with the salt, and one heaping tablespoon of sugar. Fold half of the egg whites gently through the rhubarb mixture, then very lightly, the last half. Spoon it gently into a souffle dish painted with melted butter and coated with sugar, and bake for 12 minutes at 400°. Present and serve immediately. To each portion, make a swirl topping of Whipped Cream. Pour over it, some of the pink rhubarb syrup.

SUMMER WINE

"Give me a bowl of wine . . .
In this I bury all unkindness."
WILLIAM SHAKESPEARE

LOOK TO THE LANDS where the sun shines hot for the most refreshing drinks for summertime. For Californians, to whom casual entertainment *al fresco* is a Latin inheritance, it is remarkable that the luscious and beautiful *Sangria* of Spain, Mexico, and South America is not better known. All of these are vineyard countries, with a bounty of fresh fruit in summertime, which, combined with red wine, very simply produces an instant answer for the *ennui* of enervating weather.

A recipe for *Sangria?* (Sometimes it is spelled *Sangrilla.*) Anyone can become an expert at his own version. The basic, guiding principles are always the same . . . good red table wine, and ripe, sweet fruit cut into bite-size pieces . . . plus ice and a pitcher. All other variations are indigenous side-tracks, which may vary according to the dictates of personal preference. Here are three routes to *Sangria* to try on your mental palate:

Sangria de Los Angeles — To the strained juice of 4 lemons and 1 large orange, add ½ cup of sugar. Cut the peel of another orange in one long, continuous spiral, leaving it attached to orange, which has been cut cleanly to the juicy interior. Put the orange with a tray of ice-cubes into a pitcher, allowing the peel spiral to hang out over the rim. Pour over the ice, a large bottle (⅘ quart) of good California red table wine. Garnish stemmed goblets half-filled with crushed ice, with thin slices of fresh lime.

Sangria de Sevilla. Segment two oranges (without membrane), peel and dice two ripe peaches, slice one banana into inch-size chunks. Sweeten with ½-cup of sugar sprinkled over fruit. Put sweetened fruit, ice, and slices of lime into a pitcher. Add one large bottle of red wine, with a splash of soda or Champagne. When well-chilled, serve in stemmed wine goblets of generous girth.

Sangria Tropical. Combine the luscious attributes of the first two, orange and lemon juice, orange segments, lime slices, diced peaches, chunks of pineapple, sliced bananas, plus slices of fresh papaya, mangoes, and melon balls of honey-dew, cantaloupe, with a tray of ice-cubes in a generous-sized glass pitcher. Muddle the fruit to release their nectars. Sweeten with simple syrup (½ cup of sugar dissolved over heat with ½ cup water, slightly reduced). Add one bottle of red table wine. Chill and pour into stemmed wine goblets. Blend *Sangria* with conversation, and spoon wine-drenched fruit for punctuation of dessert.

There is no harm in lending *Sangria* a few thimbles of brandy, or splashing it with Champagne, or even experimenting with a few drops of exotic *orgeat* . . . almond syrup. Ripe, sweet apricots, or sliced strawberries are a part of our indigenous summertime bounty and will also enhance *Sangria's* appeal. A word of caution. For more than four persons, two bottles of red wine are in order . . . it sips so good!

Reportedly, there is a new vogue among the health and figure-conscious members of the jet set, for Champagne and orange juice, known as *Mimosa*. The refreshing charms of this classic combination reach from the posh Factory in West Hollywood to the Runaway Bay Club in Miami, but no matter where, including the backyard shade of the San Fernando Valley, from brunch to bedtime, *freshly squeezed* orange juice and Champagne has a glowing *chic* in tall tulip glasses. Nothing is "as good as" . . . *nihil simile est idem* . . . "nothing similar is the same" . . . frozen orange juice won't make it, but our good California Champagne will! The better the Champagne, the better the *Mimosa*. Proportions? Half and half. Floating ice-cubes are not ruled out.

The piquant charms from zest of orange, sprayed over Lillet Vermouth on-the-rocks, the jet-squirt being ignited with a match, from a quick pinched cut of peel, flames this light left-bank favorite of Ernest Hemingway into smart summertime *apértif* service.

For an opening to a summertime luncheon, or leisurely evening dinner, precede dining with deep-chilled, dry California Rhine Wine. Hours before the guests arrive, place stemmed crystal wine glasses in the freezer. At the moment of service, bring them out, frosted, drop a plump strawberry in each and pour the cold wine into the pink-cloudy glass. Paul Masson's Emerald Dry is ideal, or the Johannisberg Riesling of Almadén, Louis Martini, or Beaulieu Vineyards.

A treasure from the private files of the Marquise de Pins, served to guests at the stately Beaulieu Vineyard garden estate in the Napa Valley, is a memorable experience which we are privileged to share with you here. Doubtless, it was a "bowle" of this genre which led Shakespeare to believe it might "bury all unkindness." There is a certain latitude permitted in its re-creation, but strawberries, peaches, and the banana are essential to this marriage with Champagne.

46

BOWLE

2 bottles BV Brut Champagne
4 or 5 medium size peaches
5 apricots (if available)
1 large banana

1½ cups strawberries
2 ounces good brandy
2 rounded Tbsp. of sugar

Cut the fruit up and put in a large bowl. Add the sugar and the brandy and 1½ cups chilled Champagne or just enough to not quite cover the fruit. Stir this and allow to marinate in the refrigerator for about two hours. Stir several times. Just before serving, add the rest of the Champagne which has been well chilled. Mix it well with the fruit mixture. Muddle. Strain it. Pour into well chilled glasses and serve immediately. This "Bowle" is delicious and refreshing before lunch or dinner.

"Dry," in association with wines has become a shibboleth among wine-snobs which all too-often robs the beverage of its natural pleasures. As a qualification for all table wines which are *de rigueur,* such pretension is as phoney as a 3-dollar bill. It would rule out one of the greatest joys of summertime, the incomparable harmony of sweet Sauternes with lusciously ripe melon. The combined juices of Semillon, Sauvignon, and Muscadelle grapes which are the traditional blending of the pride of France, Chateau d'Yquem, are used in premium California wineries to produce "Chateau" Sauternes types of which our State may have considerable pride, and consumers, a welcome economy of price. Again . . . nothing similar is the same . . . but when you pour iced draughts of Christian Brothers Chateau La Salle, as you serve cold wedges of California Crenshaw melon for dessert, you'll feel gratitude for the skill of Brother Timothy who made this unique wine. If you can imagine crushing a bunch of cold, sweet-ripe grapes right into your mouth, you can imagine the essence of this wine, which carries at the same time, the haunting perfume of ancient Persian Muscadelle vines.

Mid-summer also brings free stone nectarines to the market-place, making possible, from Mandarin Chinese cuisine, a luxury-for-dessert with imperial elegance. The adaptation is our own:

NECTARINES AU FROMAGE

Select the most perfect, plump, and *ripe* freestone Nectarines. With the tip of a sharp paring knife, slit the fruit to the pit along the natural seam, just enough to allow removal of the pit. Fill the cavity with a blended cream cheese, made by mixing Philadelphia cream cheese, with a little sugar, a speck of salt, two or three drops of almond extract, a tablespoon of Kirsch. When each nectarine has been filled neatly, and re-closed, wrap each in waxpaper, twisting the gathered ends to make tight closure. Chill in the refrigerator several hours. To serve, unwrap, and slice crosswise, through the cheese. Arrange on individual serving dessert plates. Garnish with piped rosettes of the cheese from a pastry bag. Serve with Port Wine.

Port Wine in summertime? Heresy to all but the knowing! But this must not be just any old Port. It has to be as rich and *liquoreuse* as you can find. No need to look further than California vineyards for such treasures either. Ficklin Tinta Port from the San Joaquin Valley is such a wine, and among their offerings of "Rarities" the Paul Masson Vineyards have two outstanding Port wines . . . Rare Tawny Port, and just making its debut, Rare Souzão Port of jeweled color, and a body which will run in rivulet "cathedral windows" when you tilt your glass to the light to enjoy even the visual sensory pleasure of this fine example of the winemaker's art.

Unless you have stood beside the sorcerer himself, right at his moving elbow, watching the magic of the golden transformation which occurs, it might not occur to you . . . but variations in formula are possible! I learned the mysteries of *Sabayon*, or as Amelio called it by its Italian name, *Zabaglione*, from the master-restaurateur himself, in San Francisco, many decades ago. We had dined late. When most of the guests of the famed peninsula-city restaurant had departed, Amelio joined us for a post-mortem of the evening. His intuition told him something more might add to the moment. Saying nothing, he merely got up from the table, beckoned for us to follow, and he walked into the kitchen. With the few efficient gestures of the expert, he gathered all he needed . . . a heavy-gauge saucepan, eggs, sugar, wine, and a wire whip. Suddenly the golden egg yolks were swimming and swirling in the pan, over heat, with sugar. When they were ribbon-smooth, he splashed in some Marsala, and then with a furtive glance, reached further, grabbing a bottle of white wine, splashing a little into the gradually thickening sauce. In what seemed only minutes, he produced a heavenly-textured confection, poured into stemmed crystal *coupes*. We returned to the table, bearing our treat with warm anticipation. But there was more than the *Zabaglione*. The moments had been a lesson in the grace of cookery, never to be forgotten.

I've repeated the formula many, many times, but when freestone peaches are at the height of their perfection in summertime, they may become the vehicle for a variation of Amelio's sorcery . . . with white wine, and a touch of lemon, as an elegant dessert.

Fresh Peaches & Summertime Sabayon

6 large freestone peaches	½ cup light white wine
6 large egg yolks	grated rind of 1 lemon
⅔ cup sugar	1 tablespoon rum
Salt	Fresh grated nutmeg

Place egg yolks and sugar in the top part of a double-boiler, or very heavy saucepan. Beat with a wire whip until the mixture is light, creamy, and fluffy. Gradually, over heat, stir in the white wine (California Semillon would be ideal). Continue stirring over the hot, but not boiling water, until the mixture thickens. If you are using the heavy saucepan, lift it from the heat occasionally. Too high temperature may cause the sauce to burn or curdle. When it has obtained the desired thickness, remove from heat, and add lemon rind, rum.

You may pour it over slightly sugared sliced peaches, either hot, or cold. The Sabayon will thicken slightly when chilled. A few gratings of fresh nutmeg is all that's needed for a final garnish.

Sangria . . . Mimosa . . . Sauterness and Melon . . . Strawberries and Rhine Wine . . . Bowle . . . Nectarines au Fromage and Port . . . these make summertime and wine an even more welcome season. Joyously, you may sing that old English verse: *"Sumer is icumen in!"*

49

RHINE WINES

Portia. Therefore, for fear of the worst, I pray thee
set a deep glass of Rhenish wine on the contrary
casket; for, if the devil be within and that
temptation without, I know he will choose it . . .
SHAKESPEARE: *The Merchant of Venice,* ACT SC. II

THE BEST WHITE WINES in the world come from the small vineyards that contour the sloping banks of the Rhine and Mosel Rivers of Germany. Roman soldiers, observing the profusion of wild vines in this northern reach of their conquest, reasoned well in sending to Italy for vineyard stock to make grapes grow for wine production . . . two thousand years ago! But the harvest in all those successive seasons has never been an easy one. Being the northernmost region of grape-growing in the world, it has also the least number of warm degree days of autumn for ripening grapes. Clusters of ripening berries hang on the vines into weather that threatens rain, frost, hail, sleet, and snow, and possible crop disaster, before the tolling church bells announce the hour of picking has arrived.

Possibly these very difficulties, including the impossibly steep terrain, yearly washed down in flooding rains, account for the excellence of the wine, by the extraordinary attention given to the vineyards, vines, grapes, and wine-making. Slate, to hold the heat of the noon-day sun through the cool nights of ripening time, must be hauled up the steep, terraced slopes, in baskets. Workers, trudging up those cliff-steep, vine-clad riverbanks, are never free of their *trag büttes,* those long wooden tubs, strapped to their backs, for carrying shale up, and grapes down these palisades. This almost inhuman labor, witnessed by Karl Marx, drove him to write his first political essay! But poets wrote about the wine! Rhenish wine was on Tudor tables in the days of all the Henrys. Elizabeth inherited a throne in danger of toppling from ruin by the mad extravagances of her father, but her economies did not include a ban on the importation of wine. Cromwell beheaded Charles I, but continued the Divine Right of Kings to have wine on the table. His frugal board supplied generous draughts of Rhenish wine. Grim fortune has never drowned the appeal of this pale golden, light, tart, flowery, crystal clear, thirst quenching wine. It is made in twelve hundred towns and villages which each counts almost two hundred

51

separate vineyard plots. One of these parishes, Hochheim, in the 19th century, produced a wine that became so popular in England, that all Rhine wines soon were dubbed "Hock" and the "Rhenish" word fell from favor. The grape from which the best wines were made, was the Riesling *(Rees'-ling)*, which, as another generic term, gained broad use.

In the 80's of the last century, when all the leading varieties of wine grapes were being imported to California from Europe, following the prodigous efforts of Count Agoston Harszthy of Buena Vista in Sonoma, Charles A. Wetmore, the State's Chief Executive Viticultural Officer, published, in the San Francisco Merchant of January 4, 1884, these comments on the German vines:

"RIESLING. — This is the noble grape *par excellence* of the Rhine, excelling in its aroma. Properly speaking, there is only one true *Riesling*, viz: That which is by courtesy called the *Johannisberg*, after one famous vineyard where it predominates. Custom has, however attached the name to other varieties, so that when we wish to speak of this genuine variety, we must now use the word *Johannisberg* to identify it. — It is an early ripener, otherwise it could not succeed on the Rhine. Experience in Europe shows that it loses its aroma and quality when cultivated in warmer countries and situations, where later ripening varieties come to perfection. On the Rhine the greatest perfection is often obtained only when the berries are left on the vines until long after the usual time of vintage. This should not be the rule here except under similar circumstances, viz: where sufficient saccharine is not obtained early. I believe that we shall not succeed in making fine Riesling wine of Rhenish type except in such places where over maturity is difficult to obtain, and where at the time of ordinary ripening the must does not exceed twenty-two per cent in sugar. What soils are not suited to the *Riesling*, we do not well know; but we do know that this variety is a failure, as to quality of wine, in the greater number of our wine-producing districts, and it is only popular in the counties north of the bay of San Francisco, and west of the Sacramento Valley. Other districts appear to be too warm or too dry for it. It would probably do well in Santa Cruz and San Mateo counties, south of the Golden Gate."

That was prophecy in 1884. Today, our highly skilled enological scientists, working in close cooperation with viticultural professionals, have temperature-charted *all* the wine-growing regions of the world, in association with planted types. In the "very cool" category of Region I, Napa, Santa Cruz, and Santa Rosa are grouped with Switzerland, the Rhine and Mosel areas, consistent with Mr. Wetmore's prediction. But even though our planting of *Johannisberg Rielsing* in properly cool areas, with attendant careful vinification, California has not yet produced a claimer to the crown of the Rhine. Golden hued, fragrant, clear, refreshing wines—*yes*, but light, fragile, delicate—*No!*

California regulations require a white table wine to be between 11% and 14% alcohol by volume. The usual European minimum is 8% or 9%. So, in one fell swoop of regulation, we knocked out the possibility of achieving equable comparison, for even our best California vintners.

Wetmore noted that "the greatest perfection is obtained only when the berries are left on the vines long after the usual time of vintage." Six hundred years ago, according to a legend shared with me by Baron Geoffrey von Mumm, of Johannisberg, at harvest time all the Rhineland villagers stood outside the gates of the fenced vineyards, listening for the steeple bells in all the onion-domed churches to proclaim the moment of picking. Day, after day dragged on. No one dared defy the law about harvesting without the Bishop of Fulda's assent. They looked at the clouds in the skies. The nights grew cold. Winds whipped off the dry leaves, leaving the shrivelling clusters. No one knew the Bishop's clerk, on his way to toll the bell, had been murdered. Finally, the news got out. No one thought those pathetic looking, withered bunches were much good, but they pressed them anyway . . . and the first *trockenbeeren-auslese*, liquoreuse molten gold wine was made! Every vintage year since, a few vineyard proprietors, with a penchant for gambling, let some grapes hang on past the harvest date, eyeing the weather, weighing the odds against rain, sleet, and snow, which might produce mold, with hopes for that concentrated essence of selected berries, nipped off, and threaded onto steel needles, harvested into special baskets for extra-special pressing. That kind of wine fetches a ransom price!

An even rarer phenomenon in German wine occurs when a sudden great temperature drop occurs, freezing the ripe grapes solid, and they can be harvested before a molding thaw destroys them. This is *Eiswein* (Ice Wine), and has only occurred ten times in the last century: 1875, 1880, 1890, 1902, 1908, 1912, 1949, 1950, 1961, and 1962. If you look, you can still find a few bottles here and there . . . for perhaps $35 or $40 each! Or more!

The terminology and nomenclature of German wines is prodigously complicated, even for an expert, once it moves beyond words into additional classifications of various colored capsules designating graduations of merit. Even casks and barrels known as *fuder* or *fass* carry separate numbers! Unless you are going to undertake a special study

53

of German wines, rely upon your wine merchant for guidance to the best bottles.

Oddly enough, wine snobs who feign tastes for nothing but dry, dry, dry wines, and will become breathless in recounting vintage tasting tales about never-to-be-had-again German wines, give themselves away to the true cognoscenti; those rare wines of memory are always *trocken-beeren-auslese*, or *beeren-auslese* (made from dried selected berries of selected bunches of late-gathered grapes) and are invariably *sweet!*

Liebfraumilch, which takes its name from the Church of Our Lady (Liebfrauenkirche) at Worms on Rhine, originally was only the wine produced from the vineyards within the shadow of that twin-spired cathedral. Today, it is a generic title for wine of the greater district. But you can still obtain wine from the small church plot under the Valkenberg "Madonna" label. Liebfraumilch of any decent vintage and bottling is ever-popular because it is an uncomplicated wine, transparent as water, light and tending toward a slight sweetness. It is, for many winemakers, a prototype because of its immense popularity.

California's truly esteemed wine scholar who holds down the chair of enology at the University of California at Davis, Maynard Anerine wrote in "Wines" published in 1965, that "many attempts to persuade producers to make some distinction between types (among generic wines. RLB) have been without success, i.e., California chablis from California rhine. Some of the wines so labeled of one company are virtually identical. Another company's products may be quite different from these and the types may be carefully distinguished." *Caveat emptor!* Let the buyer not only be aware, but guided to the better winemakers. We have done so in these pages.

This being a chapter devoted to Rhine-types, which includes, of course, Riesling, we should point out the Hallcrest Vineyard in the cool Santa Cruz mountains, and the Emerald Dry Riesling of Paul Masson, which is not strictly dry, but utterly delightful, well chilled, from a new hybrid varietal of the Riesling vine, developed at Davis. Wente Brothers Grey Riesling proves what skilled winemaking can accomplish with a lesser, usually neutral grape. Buena Vista accomplishes similar triumphs with the Green Hungarian and Gewurz-traminer grapes from Rhenish origins. Almadén, Beaulieu, Martini, Inglenook, and Christian Brothers are justifiably proud of their Johannisberg Riesling, so are Korbel, Charles Krug, Llords & Elwood, and Weibel. As a special treat for favored guests, instead of fiery cocktails before an important dinner, serve a California Johannisberg Riesling, well iced, poured into glasses kept all day in your freezer. Take them out, plop a long-stemmed strawberry into each glass, then pour cold wine splashing over them. Just to look at these pink-glowing glasses with their silver-gold nectar within is refreshment! For this privilege in California, we have a spiritual debt to the Rhineland . . . also for many advanced techniques and machinery of winemaking. This is a region of winemaking in which the wines cannot be compared in any hands-across-the-seas gesturing. They are different, but enjoyable in their individual merits, as are all wines to the true connoisseur.

Classic companion of Rhenish wines . . . either from the Rhine, Mosel, — or California . . . is salmon. Admittedly time and care are required here, but the results prove the effort valid.

POACHED SALMON STEAKS, MOUSSELINE
(4 servings)

4 center cut slices	*Court-Bouillon:*
Royal Chinook Salmon	6 cups water
1 large fresh lemon	½ bottle dry white wine
2 cucumbers, peeled, halved lengthwise, seeded, sliced on a diagonal	1 large onion, sliced
	2 carrots, sliced
Salt & Pepper	2 stalks celery, with leaves, sliced
Cherry Tomatoes, for garnish	1 bay leaf
	1 herb bouquet: Parsley, thyme, rosemary

Place all ingredients for Court-bouillon in a container large enough to hold the four fillets of salmon; bring to a boil; skim; lower the heat and simmer for 30 minutes. Strain; return clear court-bouillon to container. Wrap each fillet of salmon in a cheese-cloth sack with "handles" that will allow you to lift the fragile flesh from its flavor-cooking liquid without falling apart. Let the fillets poach in the court-bouillon that is barely simmering. When it is done, after about 15 to 20 minutes, with the help of the handles, carefully lift the steaks, possibly with a perforated spatula, drain, unwrap, skin, and remove center-bone.

SAUCE MOUSSELINE

You may serve the salmon either hot or cold. For Sauce Mousseline, blend equal parts of Hollandaise with stiffly whipped cream, stirring in a double-boiler carefully until the sauce is blended and heated through. Rectify seasoning and serve over fillets of salmon. Prepare cucumbers with French dressing, ice, and slivered onion, if the salmon is served cold; if served hot, glaze cucumbers by simmering in ¾ cup water, with 2 tablespoons sugar, 2 tablespoons butter, salt and pepper until all liquid is reduced and cucumbers are semi-transparent and glazed.

Garnish with sliced lemon, cherry tomatoes, and sauce Mousseline, piped, if you like in flourishing borders.

SAUTERNES

"Sweet compulsion flowing from the wine . . . warms the heart, and hope of Love returned, all mingled with the gifts of Dionysus darts through the brain, sending the thoughts of men to heights supreme . . ." Wine-lucid dreams of glory growing from golden draughts of wine written more than two thousand years ago by a lyric poet of Greece, survived on papyrus. We even know his name, this first "Walter Mitty" whose odes, from precious fragments, link that day with this. Rival to Pindar, Bacchylides carved his niche of immortality with the poetic skill of simple imagery. That good wine gives grace of mind is as true today as then. *"Straightway it overthrows the battlements of cities, and every man dreams that he is heir to a throne. With gold, yea, and ivory, his house is gleaming, and wheat-laden ships bring him from Egypt over the flashing sea, wealth beyond count. Thus does the drinker's heart leap with fancies."*

While no wine of Bacchylides' day survives, nor any Opimian vintages known to Pliny, nor the Coan wine of Cato, we have their glowing words they used to sing in praise of wine, along with a few antique handbooks used for making wine in ancient Greece and Rome. Our heritage in California bestows this kind continuum upon us in generous measure. For almost anyone, the place to begin its enjoyment is with the brilliant golden-crystal wine we call *Sauterne*.

The name comes from France. Sauternes (spelled with a final "s") is one of the principal communes of Bordeaux, lying west and south of the river Garonne. The pebbly soil and subsoil in combination with a climatological phenomenon involving high humidity during the ripening time of grapes, has produced through many centuries, a wine of curious and delightful sweetness. Many chateaux in the Sauternes district produce this elixir of the grape, but supreme above all, is that from the Chateau d'Yquem. The wines of the French Sauternes will have a range of from 4 to 6 per cent residual grape-sugar sweetness, suggesting service with the fresh ripe fruits of summertime as dessert. It is traditionally chilled to control the cloying quality of its sweetness. But to countless palates through the ages, nothing mars the luscious richness of its flavor, nor the refined delicacy of its fragrance. These seductive charms appeal to the initiate in wine experience, and to the seasoned connoisseur.

57

Taste, in wine, as in food, music, or any of the art forms, is a complex development which often follows a constant course. This *learning-curve* begins with that which is the most easily recognized and understood, progressing to more subtle and complex forms of address for mental synthesis. Wine appeals first to the *eye* . . . for color, brilliance and clarity, then to the *nose* . . . for bouquet and definitive fragrance, the *tongue* . . . for taste, and the *mouth* . . . detecting body and viscosity, and finally, that lingering melody of aroma we call *after-taste*, haunting all the olefactory apparatus simultaneously. One taste alerts, in a symphony of stimuli, a multi-organ response. So, we have the scientifically accurate term for wine-tasting, a technical tongue-twister . . . *organoleptic evaluation!* Mr. Webster says: *"Making an impression on an organ of special sense."*

California Sauterne, because it is directly beautiful to the eye, delicate in flavor, and slightly sweet, is easily the most popular table wine in America. From marketing experience, our wineries produce a drier Sauterne than the French, in a range of sweetness from a negligible 0.25 per cent sugar in *Dry Sauterne*, 1 to 3 per cent for *Sauterne* and *Haut Sauterne*, and as high as 3 to 6 per cent in the sweetest examples, which always bear the winery name in a tradition which flatters Chateau d'Yquem by nominal imitation, giving us our own estate-bottled Chateau Beaulieu, Chateau La Salle, Chateau Concannon, Chateau Novitiate, Chateau Masson, and Chateau Wente.

French traditions in the making of Sauterne in California had a most illustrious beginning. Cuttings of the three principal grape varieties . . . *Semillon, Sauvignon Blanc,* and *Muscatel de Bordelais*, which, in a field-blend compose the wine of Chateau d'Yquem, were presented by the Chateau to the first California Viticultural Commission in the early 80's of the last century, for planting in the gravelly soil of the Livermore Valley. To the untrained eye, this coarse rocky earth would not suggest agriculture of any kind, but the minerals and drainage are not only ideal for these vines, but the rocks become a reservoir of the sun's heat through the long cold nights.

Historic El Mocho vineyard, which contains the mother vines brought from France, was visited by the late Marquis de Lur Saluces, owner of Chateau d'Yquem, in 1941, as guest of the Wente Brothers owners of the celebrated land. This was twenty-six years ago, but I was standing beside the Marquis, in the Wente tasting room, as he told his hosts: "I am glad to see my 'children' doing so well in California. I'm proud to known them in this setting where they are so well cared for."

At luncheon with many Livermore Valley winemakers, cultivating descendant vines from his French estate, he found them all brilliant heirs to the name of his native commune . . . Sauternes!

Enological (wine-making) technology in California is unequaled anywhere in the world today. Among all of our good wines, differences exist, principally due to variations in the three components basic to any wine-making: vineyard location, grape varieties, vinting technology. So you may well expect to find the Sauterne of one region, one wine-maker quite unlike the Sauterne of another. Chateau Wente of the golden Livermore Valley, known as "the Sauterne district of America" smacks of the sun and soil of that Bay region. Chateau La Salle, of the Christian Brothers, high in the hills of the Napa Valley, is totally different, but equally elegant. You will pay dearly for Cresta Blanca Premier Semillion, made with prodigous expense and humidity control to re-create the "noble rot" fungus spore of *Botrytis cinerea*, which in France, make Sauternes a liquoreuse wine. It was a noble experiment, with noble results, producing, in limited quantity golden proof of California's potential. It is deliberately sweet and rich! Dry Sauterne is deliberately without sweetness. Somewhere on the range between, you may find your place on your own learning curve of wine-taste. You will also find the drier examples compliment fish, chicken and lobster, while the sweetest are incomparable companions for luscious bowls of fresh sliced peaches, chilled ripe honeydew melon tumbling with blueberries, and classic punctuation for lofty-domed dessert soufflés.

Each of these wineries produces a variety of shimmering Sauternes: Almadén, Beaulieu, Beringer, Buena Vista, Christian Brothers, Concannon, Cresta Blanca, Guild, Italian Swiss Colony, Korbel, Chas. Krug, Louis M. Martini, Novitiate of Los Gatos, Paul Masson, Sebastiani, Weibel, and Wente Brothers.

A small investment in your local wine emporium will give you a dozen bottles for taste-adventuring and discovery, and allow equal economy in experiments in the kitchen with the "bird and bottle". Here are three different ways to approach this promise of pleasure.

BACHELOR GOURMET
BIRD AND BOTTLE RECIPE FILE

Miraculously easy, dramatically colorful, quick without sacrificing flavor, this casserole will make no demands on punctuality of the table-hour! It can rest in its juices!

Poulet Macedoine

2½ to 3lb. frying chicken disjointed
1 no. 2 tin Fruits for Salad
1 pkg. Instant Meat Marinade (Adolph's)

⅔ cup California Sauterne
1 ounce Curacao or Triple Sec (optional)

Pour contents of package of Instant Meat Marinade into shallow pan. Blend thoroughly with syrup drained from can of fruit salad (approx. ⅔ cup). Place chicken pieces in Marinade. Pierce deeply and thoroughly with a fork to carry flavor deep down and insure true juiciness. Turning frequently, marinate 15 minutes. Carefully arrange marinade-coated pieces of chicken in casserole. Place in pre-heated 350° oven for 45 minutes, without cover. Remove casserole and arrange fruit over browned chicken. To remaining marinade, add ⅔ cup Sauterne. Blend and pour over chicken. Cover and return to oven for 10 minutes. Just before serving, add one ounce of Curacao. Serve with Quick Rice pilaf. *(Note: If a thicker sauce is desired, thicken with 2 tablespoons of cornstarch, simmering until thick and semi-transparent.)*

Rainy Sunday Chicken-in-a-pot

4 to 5 pound roasting chicken
4 carrots, peeled, split long
2 leeks, pared and split
4 onions, peeled and quartered
4 celery branches, with tops
6 mushrooms
½ cup Sauterne

2 turnips, peeled, quartered
1 tablespoon salt
Fresh ground pepper
¼ teasp. each Thyme, Basil, Sage
1 cup minced parsley
1 sliver lemon peel
½ teaspoon Ac'cent

In a large heavy pot, make a bed of the vegetables. Place the whole chicken upon it in enough water to cover ⅔ of the chicken. Add remaining ingredients. Cover. Allow to come to a boil, then turn down heat and simmer gently for 50 minutes, or until breast of chicken is spongy to touch. Remove Chicken to serving casserole with a little broth and keep warm. Strain vegetables from broth, saving whole pieces for serving. Reduce broth, for making sauce.

Veloute Sauce

3 tablespoons butter or margarine
4 tablespoons flour
1 cup heavy cream

3 egg yolks
1 cup strained chicken broth

In a heavy saucepan, over low heat, blend butter and flour, and stir until smooth, 3 or 4 minutes. Add heated chicken stock slowly, lifting from heat, stirring until smooth and of proper thick consistency. Blend egg yolks with cream. Add to sauce slowly, partially, until all is absorbed into sauce. Taste and correct seasonings. Simmer to correct thickness, *but do not allow it to boil.* Serve with carved chicken and garnish of vegetables.

From the pages of classic French cuisine comes this age-old tech-que, all but forgotten in our freeze-foil-bake era. It makes use of an every-day, plain-Jane, Kraft paper bag (no printing please) greased generously, folded at the opening, stapled, and placed mid-oven on the wire shelf. Like, how easy can it be!

POULET EN PAPILLOTE

3 lb. chicken, whole	1 cup prepared dressing, crumbed
2 tablespoons butter	1 shallot
¼ cup minced parsley	1 onion, minced
1 can Consomme Madrilene	2 pkg. unflavored gelatine
1 can Chicken Consomme onion	Salt & pepper

Mix butter and parsley with prepared dressing. Place half inside the bird with giblets. Grease paper bag inside, generously. With seam-side up, place remaining half of crumbs, as bed for chicken. Fold over ends securely, and staple. Place bag gently in pre-heated 300° oven for 1½ hours. Add gelatine to consomme, blend and chill, pouring each separately onto cookie sheets to chill. Dice fine as bed for roast chicken, with added parsley garnish. Serve hot or cold.

CHABLIS

No SENSIBLE MAN ever ate a piece of flint. But neither has anyone ever come up with a vocabulary which is capable of transmitting verbally, the complex sensations of taste. So we limp along in the vague realms of figurative speech, describing wines with words of hopeful meaning. Cognoscenti of the wine world invariably punctuate their praise of a fine French Chablis by concluding that it has a taste of *gunflint!* This driest of all great white table wines, classic companion to oysters-on-the-half-shell, does indeed have a unique, clean, sharp and refreshing taste, but to describe it as *"flinty"* begs the issue . . . *reductio ad absurdum!*

To sharpen the semantic focus upon *Chablis* and its *taste* requires separate consideration. The wine itself is clouded with ambivalence. Properly speaking, Chablis (pronounced: *shab-leé*), is the wine made from grapes grown on the chalk-hills in and around the village of Chablis, a separate area of Burgundy, the *département* of Yonne, 110 miles south-east of Paris. The slate-roofed village banks a small river, La Serein, which flows into the Yonne, and then into the Seine . . . a route which allowed the golden, green-hued wine to reach the French court in centuries past. The product of Cistercian monks working the difficult terrain gained early fame. It was described poetically as having "the color of spring water in sunlight" . . . "sometimes golden, which has aroma and body, an exquisite savor and fills the heart with joyous assurance." These words, written by a Cistercian monk in 1280, are still accurate description. Demand for the wine of Chablis long ago out-distanced the supply, and was responsible for the most outrageous faking. Genuine Chablis comes from only about thirty small vineyards on either side of the River Serein, comprising less than two thousand planted acres. By French law, only one grape is cultivated for Chablis . . . the shy-bearing *Pinot Chardonnay,* the same grape which makes the "divine" Montrachet and Meursault further south along the rolling hills of the Burgundian Côte d'Or. Chablis of officially controlled designation as Great Growths (*Grands Crus*) are always sold and labelled with the proud vineyard name, and there are only

63

eight of them: Blanchots . . . Bougros . . . Les Clos . . . Grenouilles . . . Les Preuses . . . Valmur . . . Vaudesir . . . and La Moutonne. There are about two dozen First Growths (*Premier Crus*) sold as Chablis lined with the vineyard name. Wine labelled merely *Chablis*, without a vineyard name, indicates a French wine from this district, but not from one of the outstanding vineyards.

Chablis . . . as one of the most famous white wines in the world, has been subject not only to imitation, but to *generic* acceptance as a *type* of wine. To the French, such misappropriation of terminology is a violation of moral law. They do not accept this kind of imitation as any kind of flattery, but all kinds of wine goes forth masquerading as *Chablis*. Some of it is pretty, and lots of it is pretty awful! The same can be said about *Champagne* . . . the word and the product. The French deny any effervescent wine not made in the Province of Champagne the right to such appellation. The American government thinks otherwise, and has accepted both Champagne and Chablis as generic terms, stipulating however, that the origin of the wine be stated in type comparably as large as the wine designated. So we have California Champagne . . . and California Chablis.

We have already indicated the best of the true French Chablis. The best California Chablis comes from the premium vineyards of the State, but as a *generic* term, no specific grape variety must be included in a *California Chablis*. The true French Chablis grape is the Pinot Chardonnay, so for the best California examples, which might have rough comparison with the French product, the wine to find is *Pinot Chardonnay!* All the rest will be white, dry, and varying greatly in all other qualities of taste according to the composition of its blending of grapes other than the noble white Pinot.

All of which leads us directly to the consideration of *taste*, and the means of describing it, most particularly, the "flinty" taste of French Chablis, being the fountainhead of its peculiar fame.

Flavor is a mingled sensation of *smelling* and *tasting*. Just as there are primary colors . . . red, yellow, and blue, from which we may make orange, green, and purple and the whole rainbow range of shadings in between . . . so there are basic and primary odors: *Spicy, Flowery, Fruity, Resinous, Burnt*, and *Foul*. Taste is reduced to four categories: *Sweet, Sour, Salty*, and *Bitter*. The *sour* taste in foods and beverages is due to the acids which are present in them, which is frequently refreshing, and thirst-quenching, like lemon-ade. In combination with sweetness, such modification makes that acidity palatable, and even more desireable when coupled with fruity or flowery fragrance! *"Appleness"* is one of the most instantly understood taste-words. But how on earth can anyone understand *"Flinty"*?

Chablis of the *Great Growths* does have a peculiar and distinctive taste, which comes from the calcareous soil of the hill-vineyards. The white, chalky hills are the spinal outcroppings of the Jura Mountain range, a system which connects France, Switzerland and Germany in easily visible evidence, and in prehistoric consideration links the chalky areas of Chablis, and Champagne with the White Cliffs of Dover! In something known to geologists as the Mesozoic era, the minute remains of marine organisms, fragments of shell, produce that calcareous substance we know as *chalk*, and when mixed with other clayey material forms an identifying band of earth stratum specifically identified as *Kimeridgian* clay. The hills surrounding the village of Chablis are not only difficult to cultivate because of their steep slopes, but because of the very thin layer of top soil which constantly is washed away by rains, and which must be carried back up in the back-breaking labor of basket-loads. As a result, many of the old true Chablis vineyards have gone out of production. The farmers' revenue was just not great enough for the dedicated labor involved, particularly when many seasons would bring disastrous rains, and frost destroying whatever meagre crops were there. All of this merely adds to the demand for the great Chablis of good years, raising its international price and availability to the general market.

The taste of wine is a complex miracle resulting from those microscopic particles of soil drawn out of the earth by the root system of the vines, into the fruit, biochemically blended with natural sugars in fermentation, balanced with natural glycerins, minerals, acids, odor-producing esters, and living yeasts. A ripe grape is almost 80 per cent water, but the rest is that divine combination, which is nowhere identical, that makes wine the complex and confoundingly difficult beverage to describe. The identifying element most predominant in true *Chablis* comes from prehistoric *Kimeridgian clay* composition of those hillside vineyards. The pale golden wine owes its *flowery fragrance* to the *Pinot Chardonnay* vine species. It is without sweetness, and totally dry because all of the sugars have been converted to alcohol. The flavor combines the taste of the component minerals in suspension, flowing in a river of sensation upon the palate. Flint? There is no evidence of it, but there are whole volumes of reference to the composition of Kimeridgian clay, naming huge extinct birds with lateral steering feathers and claws on their wings, reptilian jaws and teeth, the Pterosauria and Pterodactyls! Palaeontologists are indebted to

Kimeridgian slate for their fossil-impressions of the oldest known bird ... *Archaeopteryx* ... winelovers need a new challenge to their vocabulary to pay their just reverential debt to the Mesozoic era. Maybe that should be the salutary word ... *Mesozoic* ... for Chablis! It does mean more than "flint". For an easy garden variety description, try "bitter apple" ... it might turn you away from this golden wine, but its sharply defined thirst-quenching acidity will do wonders to cut through the oiliness of fish cooked simply *à la meunière*. Well-chilled, even lesser Chablis has a natural marine harmony with oysters which seems divinely inspired ... and paleontologically correct!

When the warm months of summer arrive, why not experiment with half a dozen or more California Chablis ... for chilled, icy-cold *apéritif* service? Put the wine and the glasses in the refrigerator in the morning, and when the pre-prandial hour arrives, bring out both, and into the frosty glasses pour the simmering pale gold wine, as dry as a Martini, but not nearly as deadly. Bounce Paul Masson's Pinot Chardonnay against Paul Masson Chablis ... in concert with Wente Brothers Livermore Valley Chablis and Wente Brothers Pinot Chardonnay. In the same top category you'll find Almadén Chardonnay and Chablis. Comparisons are educational. You'll find Beaulieu Vineyards, Christian Brothers, and Louis Martini examples from the Napa Valley are priced much higher than other bottles of Chablis on the market shelf. One taste, and you'll know why. One fine day, you may find a bottle of French Chablis Valmur or Chablis Vaudésir, with its Kimeridgian flavor. The Jurassic system touched North America. Who knows but what we may have some Mesozoic clay in coastal California vineyards? Our better California Chablis is truly superb ... with the pedigree of premium vintners for quality insurance ... when you buy.

Filets de Soles au Chablis

Simplicity is the key to this straight-forward recipe. It may be used with fillets of local sole, Dover Sole, or Sand-Dabs, the delicacy of flavor arising from the wine, herbs, and concentrated essence of both in the reduced *fumet*, as the sauce.

Place the fillets of sole, rolled or folded, in a well-buttered, heat-proof *gratin* dish, or shallow casserole. Sprinkle them with finely chopped shallots, minced with parsley, crumbled thyme, salt and pepper. Pour over them, sufficient California Chablis to cover, and two or three tablespoons of water. Cover with buttered aluminum foil and bake in a moderate oven (375°) for about 15 minutes. Arrange the poached fillets on a heated serving dish, and keep hot. Pour off the *fumet* into a small saucepan and reduce over high heat to half the original quantity. Beat into it, with a wire whisk, 4 tablespoons of butter. Season to taste, and pour over fillets of sole, garnishing with finely minced parsely, and if you wish, whole sauteed, fluted mushrooms and lemon wedges.

Quiche à l'Oignon

1 cup sliced, mild yellow onions	2 cups rich milk (part cream)
2 tablespoons butter or margarine	1 teaspoon salt
½ pound Swiss Gruyere cheese, grated	¼ teaspoon pepper
4 strips crisp bacon, crumbled	¼ teaspoon fresh grated nutmeg
3 whole eggs, beaten	1 unbaked, single crust 9-inch pie shell

Saute onions in butter until golden, transparent, and soft. Mix with the grated cheese and crumbled bacon, and spoon into pie-shell. Combine the remaining ingredients and pour over the cheese and onions. Bake in a pre-heated moderate oven (350°) for 45 minutes, or until a silver knife blade, when inserted, comes out clean. Allow to settle for two or three minutes, and serve, hot. Six servings.

VIN ROSE

"Vin rosé . . . toujours à propos"

IN THE BOOK OF SNOBS, none is more apparent than the counterfeit connoisseur who looks down his nose at *vin rosé*. Snobbism is an attitude without education. Pink wine, made by a master *vigneron* in any wine country of the world, brings to the bowl of its crystal cup, the most delicate revelation of its varietal origins. It can be Grenache, Gamay, Grignolino, Cabernet Sauvignon, or even Pinot Noir. It may be fragrant and still, sparkling with the effervescence of Champagne, or merely threading a piquant *insouciance* of bubbling called "crackling". The olefactory sense of the true connoisseur is capable of distinguishing between four to ten thousand different odors! Even an educated amateur, through experience, can train his nose in the discovery of vinous merit. All but a popular few pink wines of the current market are worthy of meritorious consideration. Even the sweetest examples have their place in a planned program of chilled pouring with summertime menus.

There's no way of knowing who made the first pink wine, but history is quite clear about the first pink Champagne! It was made by the venerable Dom Pérignon in the cellar of his abbey in Epernay. All of the wines of the Champagne region had a tendency to develop a sparkle, no matter whether they came from white grapes or black. The good abbot, as we all know, stoppered some bottles with hemp which imprisoned the bubbles, and months later, the young white wine he had made from black grapes, erupted from the mouth of the bottle in a foaming extravagance which has not stopped in three hundred years! In the beginning . . . it was pink! The white juice of black grapes, left even momentarily on the pigment-rich skins, drew color from the crushed mass, before being drawn off to complete its fermentation. A happy accident perhaps, worthy of such an auspicious beginning.

Most *vin rosé*, despite the opinions of ding-a-ling wine-snobs have differentiating character. This comes from the tannin borrowed from the black skins of the variety of grape from which they are made. The smaller amount than exists in the full red wine, allows and permits a quicker market readiness. Truly a creative product of the winemaker,

69

its depth of color depends totally upon the desire of the winemaker and how long he wishes to leave the fermenting juice "on the skins." In its complex, he can use all black grapes, or a combination of both. Or he can blend it from red and white wines. He can make it dry, or sweet, still, sparkling, or crackling.

There's no denying the popularity of the artificially carbonated crackling crock from Portugal. To millions of Americans who grew up on soda pop, it has the instant familiarity of the known sensation, in a sophisticated wrapper. Who cares whether or not it's a great wine? To those who love it, the price is right, and twenty wholesale dealers in Los Angeles alone will tell you so. They all carry it like a grocer who sells sugar, soap, flour, and salt. It's basic to the trade.

Beyond this basic crock, however, is a whole realm of rosé wines inviting your most discriminating attention, even searching expedition. Should summertime find you flying to Italy, take time out to drive south of Naples, the winding coastal cliffs of Amalfi, through the vineyards of Lacrima Christi, to the terraced hills of Ravello overlooking the Gulf of Salerno and the islands of Capri. Richard Wagner composed the celestial music of *Parsifal* here, and without doubt, sipped the amethyst-pink Caruso wine with its fragrance of lilacs. Right here, in California, if you look for it, you can discover the Cretan wines of Greece, a dry Minos Rosé, legendary wines of Cypress once served in the golden cups of kings! But Europe cannot properly claim any edge. The Lancer's may have the edge in Portuguese export, but a novice nose can find more vinous pleasure in the handsome squat oval bottle of Mateus Still Rosé, with its dignified and decorative label.

Southern California wineries seldom get a tumble in premium wine table talk, but when the subject of pink wines is due, so is mention of Grignolino Rosé, estate-bottled in Etiwanda by Regina. The Italian grape produces its own spicy charm and pink-orange hue.

Dominating the production of pink wine in California, is the full-blown beauty deriving from the Grenache grape of Tavel, France. Almadén, Beaulieu, Buena Vista, Christian Brothers Italian Swiss Colony, Charles Krug, Paul Masson, San Martin, Sebastiani, Souverain, and Weibel winemakers all produce this varietal example, but in their own varying degrees of excellence of bouquet and degree of dryness. Louis M. Martini and the Heck Brothers of Korbel on the Russian River find the exceptional fruitiness of the Gamay of France's Beaujolais produces a youthful freshness you will most enjoy in this popular pink.

Two wineries gambled with their jewels of the vineyard, the

Cabernet Sauvignon, and won! The Rosebrook of Buena Vista, and Rose of Cabernet of Llords & Elwood establish new heights of character and depth of taste sensation in *vin rosé*. A story I've been fond of telling for almost ten years illustrates well, the very existence of this wine. Cabernet Sauvignon, native grape of Bordeaux, used in making the aristocratic Clarets of the great Chateaux, is, in the opinion of all the experts, the most prized red wine grape from France because of its superb adaptability to California soil and climate. It not only makes our best red wine, but it fetches the highest price on the grape market. Once budded to native American root-stock, the winemaker must wait a good five or six years before he can expect a measurable crop for testing the wisdom of his planting, and another two years to evaluate his wine. That's a long and expensive time! The waiting years had passed for Frank Bartholomew, United Press International head-man, who had acquired the historic vineyard property. He had employed the skilled assistance of André Tchelistcheff, enologist of Beaulieu Vineyards, in the production of his Buena Vista wines. Now the first prideful gathering of Cabernet Sauvignon was at hand. Tchelistcheff calmly suggested he would like to make a rosé wine with the Cabernet harvest! It could only be likened to a suggestion by your jeweler that you allow your diamonds to be ground into dust to to make glitter for your Christmas cards! Gulping hard, Bartholomew gave consent and the wine was made . . . the first Cabernet Rosé in California . . . but what a wine! The color was the pure pink of a garden rose, with matching fragrance. In its shimmering depth, the regal worth of breed boldly proclaimed itself. The limited supply soon developed a waiting list. There's no longer any hesitation about making pink wine with Cabernet Sauvignon at Buena Vista! Richard and Mike Elwood can be equally proud of their Rose of Cabernet from their young vineyard-winery in the Santa Clara Valley at Fremont.

California is not outdone by either Portugal or France in sparkling varieties of *vin rosé*, either. Paul Masson Crackling Rosé is a *natural* wine of capricious, deserved popularity, bottle-fermented like fine champagne.

Connoisseurs are apt to be disdainful of sweet or sparkling wines with reason, if the bubbles or sugar are used to masquerade otherwise undistinguished wine. A simple, dry wine, either red, white, or pink, must stand solely on the merits of its *vinous* attributes of color, bouquet, and flavor. For Cabernet Sauvignon, or the equally rare noble import from the Cote d'Or of Burgundy, of Clos Vougeot and Romanée-Conti, this is traditional. There is daring extravagance in making a pink sparkling wine with Pinot Noir for an American market. It could not be inexpensive, but it could be superlative to drink. André Tchelistcheff did it seasons ago. Limited in quantity like all gems of worth, it made a quiet debut . . . *Champagne Rosé de Pinot Noir* from Beaulieu Vineyards of the Napa Valley. When I first tasted it, at the winery, chilled and foaming the surface with its small pearl bubbles, I reached for words to describe its stateliness and consumate elegance. "It's like a beautiful woman in a satin opera gown," I said. The sensitive Russian-born winemaker replied in philosophical terms endemic among winelovers, "A beautiful woman can only be a beautiful woman if she brings you understanding as a man." This is but one of the joys of wine, ephemeral, defying definition, but like every universally popular vin rosé . . . *toujours à propos!*

How should you serve it? And when? With what? Always well-chilled to refreshing coldness. It is superb as a luncheon wine complimenting either fish, poultry, lamb or any kind of meat casseroles. Drawn from a *weinheber,* as shown in the illustrating photograph, it mingles with conversation, fruit and cheese long past dessert. Much of the pleasure of wine is in finding the one that most appeals to you. The shelves of your local wine emporium are lined with inexpensive invitations to *vin rosé*, from California, well worth accepting frequently.

Gigot de Printemps aux Mirepoix

One of the luxuries of springtime marketing in America, particularly in the West, is the availability of young lamb. This is one of the most certain ways of presenting a young leg of lamb roasted to the most savory delicacy, taking its cue from classic meat cookery, and the use of a bed of aromatic vegetables, which also serve to give richness to a simple "pan sauce."

1 leg of lamb, skinned
Salt and freshly ground pepper
Ac'cent
1 clove garlic, pressed
Juice of 1 lemon
¾ cup finely chopped parsley
3 tablespoons breadcrumbs
2 teaspoons thyme

For the Mirepoix:

3 carrots, peeled, diced

3 stalks of celery, minced
1 white onion, minced
2 cups chicken stock
1 cup dry white wine

Beurre manie:

1 tbsp. butter
1 tbsp. flour
blend together with fingers
to form a ball.

Pre-heat oven to 300°.

Make a light paste of the parsley, lemon juice, breadcrumbs, salt,

72

pepper, accent, garlic. Make incisions into the lamb with a sharp knife, and force some of this mixture into them. With the remainder, spread it over the surface of the meat. Insert a meat thermometer. Place it on a rack, in a low shallow roasting pan, to which you have added around and over the lamb, the mixed vegetables of the mirepoix. Place all in the oven. Baste every 20 minutes with the wine and chicken stock together, until meat thermometer registers 180. Remove, and keep warm (Cooking time: approx. 40 minutes per pound). Drain off all pan juices, and strain. Pour into sauce-pan. Remove excess fat from the top, and thicken with beurre manie. Rectify seasoning with salt, pepper, wine.

Many a roast is ruined by over-cooking. A meat thermometer is the best insurance. We have suggested taking the roast lamb from the oven when the interior temperature reaches 180°. As the meat continues cooking slightly even after being removed from the oven, the roast will still be pink inside . . . as it should be.

Carving lamb presents two methods . . . cross grain, into the bone, in the American style, or horizontally, in thin slices in the French manner. We prefer the latter. Delicately thin slices then run with juices, and should the meat have even a slight tendency to toughness, it will be minimized.

CLARET

THE SEARCH AFTER CLARET

Julius Caesar
Decimus Magnus Ausonius
Charlemagne
Eleanor of Aquitaine
Henry Plantagenet
Richard Coeur de Lion
Joan of Arc
Louis XIV
Richelieu
Countess Dubarry
Madame de Pompadour
Charles II of England
Samuel Pepys
Talleyrand
Baron Rothschild
Étienne Thée
Charles Lefranc
Paul Masson
Count Agoston Haraszthy
Georges de Latour
Maynard Amerine
Frank Schoonmaker

FEW THINGS IN LIFE bring more joyous satisfaction than a good dinner and a good bottle of wine to go with it! The imposing cast of historical figures forming the masthead of this story have an awesome magnitude, but their simple humanity is happily apparent in the unceasing search after Claret, the wonderful red wine of the *Cabernet Sauvignon* grape! The story of the vine and the lands where it could prosper best, is the fabric of history itself, the tapestry of civilization.

The story of Claret begins in one of the three divisions of Gaul, when Julius Caesar claimed, as part of his far-flung empire, the vineyard region now known as Bordeaux, then already productive with vines, a seeming-Paradise called *Aquitania.* These were the good times of the Roman Empire, its consuls and governors carrying the exchange of commerce and education from the Eternal City to the most remote outposts of Britain. But in that part of Gaul lying between the Pyrenees and the Garonne, a fourth century scribe extolled the vines, the rivers, the meadows and the woods of Aquitaine, of which the inhabitants seemed "to have been given an image of Paradise rather than a part of Gaul." Life within the walled city of Burdigala (Bordeaux) was one of ordered provincialism, a center of education. The Consul of the city, a native Roman, Decimus Magnus Ausonius, poet and rhetorician, had been tutor to the imperial court, for the education of Gratian, but following the murder of the youthful Caesar, returned to his Saint Emilion vineyards, spending his autumn years in cultivation of those midnight-blue grapes, whose small clusters made wines superior to any the imperial court had ever known . . . lighter, softer, jeweled in color, in contrast to the heavy Mediterranean wines. Wine is still made in the rocky hills which were the site of the Roman Consul's villa and vineyard . . . This is Château Ausone, of Saint Emilion . . . where the vine has had its ruby yield in each of two thousand years.

Aquitaine was a prize fief of Charlemagne, which he bestowed upon his son, Louis, as a separate Carolingian kingdom in 781, but the vineyard realm enters its greatest vinous significance when the whole territory moved, as a dowry of the daughter of William X, when Eleanor of Aquitaine became the wife of Louis VII, king of France.

The English traditions of Claret begin with one of the stormiest separations and marital histories in Christendom. Eleanor bore Louis VII two daughters, but even more malice. That he led the 2nd Crusade against the Saracen infidels evoked only her displeasure, and in his absence, she found comfort and support in the company of Henry Plantagenet, direct descendant of William the Conqueror, and heir to the throne of England. In 1152, the not-so-gentle Eleanor (played in an excellent film "A Lion in Winter" by Katherine Hepburn) divorced Louis, married Henry, bore him five sons and three daughters. The eldest son, John, John, and his brother Richard, who was to become known as "The Lion-Hearted", people the dramas of those days . . . the Crusades, and the Hundred Years War, between England and France, set off by the marital move of Eleanor, sweeping the whole of Aquitaine under the crown of England, and Henry II. Bordeaux was an English possession until the 15th century, and the good red wine, which the English called *claret*, deriving from the French word *clair*, meaning light and clear (as apposed to the darker wines of Burgundy), traveled across the Channel in continuous, duty-free traffic. The taverns of Londontown, and the cellars of every castle boasted the best of the antique province of Aquitaine, now known as Guienne and Gascony.

The generous flow of wine was checked in the 15th century, which saw French resistance against the English intrigues with the Dukes of Burgundy, rise to battle, led by the Maid of Orleans, Joan of Arc, concluding with her martyrdom, at Rouen on May 30th, 1431. French victories over the English at Normandy and Guienne, in 1453 returned the allegiance of old Aquitania to France. Strong prejudice affected the cross-channel trade in wine, and smuggling kept the taverns supplied for the next two centuries, to satisfy the English demand. Quarrels between Charles II of England by the trade policies of Louis XIV's minister, the Marquis Colbert, was met with a prohibition on the import of all wines from France. England turned to Portugal, the land of their new queen, for red wine. Jonathan Swift, Defoe, Samuel Pepys, and Richard Ames wrote reams of verse, satire, panegyrics in praise of Claret, scorching comments on the "red Port of Portugal growth!" Richard Ames "Search after Claret" sold two editions printed in paperback in 1691. But Claret remained in France, as "Richelieu's tea" and the châteaux of Bordeaux became the pet endowments of the Court of the Louis. For the sumptuous banquets of the Sun-King at Versailles: Madame de Pompadour sought the wines of the pebbled vineyards of Lafite along the Gironde. The brother-in-law of the reigning favorite of Louis XV, the Countess Dubarry did as much for . . . Château Margaux, at the elegant court.

The French Revolution saw an exchange of proprietorship in many of the great estates, but their sale by the state landed them again into traditional hands. One of the early 19th century owners of the illustrious Chateau Haut Brion was no less than the celebrated diplomat, Talleyrand, whose table was served by Caréme, the chef of kings, and the king of chefs.

Revival of the English trade came after the Revolution of 1789, with a return to the exchange of commerce and tourists. By the time of Gladstone, in 1860 the duty on French wine was reduced to one shilling per gallon, and once more the Bordeaux ruby became the bright jewel in every Englishman's prideful cellar. The wines of Bordeaux had come full circle to Eleanor of Aquitaine's decision to marry the youthful English Prince, Henry Plantagenet. The time between had created "Port Wine", and England's taste for wine made it the enviable market it remains today.

The importation of some American rootstock to French botanical gardens in 1858 carried disaster. The vines were infected with a plant-louse called *phylloxera*. They spread through the vineyards of Europe like a cinder in a dry wheat-field, creating unparalleled destruction. The great estates of Bordeaux and Burgundy were reduced to withered stubble. Time, and grafting whole new vineyards onto phylloxera-resistant, hardy, native American root-stock would rebuild the dominions of the vine, but the economic upheaval produced side-effects, in the emigration of many vineyardists to the New World, carrying the traditions of fine winemaking with them.

The Gold Rush of '49 in California, was followed by a Grape Rush in the 50's. When the news of the phylloxera disaster in Europe threatened depletion of that wine-supply, California emerged as a potiential vineyard for the world market. Prices on vineyard real estate soared. But of the thousands of acres planted, only those tended by men of generations in wine thrived and survived. At a place called New Almadén, in the Santa Clara Valley, beside the Guadalupe Creek, named by Spanish settlers after the town of Almadén in Spain, where quicksilver was mined, a young Frenchman, interested in vines, and not the available quicksilver, set out a vineyard. He was Étienne Thée. In 1852, another Frenchman, Charles Lefranc, joined him, as a neighbor, and married Thée's daughter. Fine wines cannot be manufactured: they depend upon nature, the grapes, the soil, sun, and devotion of the winemaker to his goal. It has been forever true. The pride of Charles Lefranc in his California vineyard, was no less than that of Decimus Magnus Ausonius at Saint Emilion. The Charles Lefranc Wine Company thrived, and with vinestock imported from France, produced its first major vintage in 1862. It was well on the road to fame when a young man from Burgundy joined them, in 1878. He was Paul Masson, born into wine traditions, at Beaune. Vineyards were the only environment he knew. His eyes took in the California landscape with a knowing vision. The oak trees crowning the gradual knolls around Los Gatos and Saratoga, on the western edge of the Santa Clara Valley, had to hold moisture! They could support vines! There he would make his own dominion, a vineyard-in-the-sky, for himself, and his bride, the daughter of Charles Lefranc. In this history, is the genesis of two of California's finest contemporary wineries . . . Almadén and Paul Masson.

The search after Claret . . . in California . . . for truly fine wines, must list two other pioneers, Count Agoston Haraszthy, the Hungarian nobleman whose dynamic career established the foundation of the California Wine Industry in a dramatic saga culminating in his own Buena Vista Vineyard, in Sonoma . . . and Georges de Latour, who came to the Napa Valley, from Bordeaux in 1900, founding the great estate flourishing in the finest traditions today, at Beaulieu Vineyards.

The search after Claret . . . in California . . . enlisted, from the last quarter of the 19th century, the dedication of the University of California to this agricultural challenge. Departments of Viticulture and Enology were established at Davis. Following the repeal of national prohibition in the United States, a new market was opened for American wines, from vineyards long dormant, or turned to more productive growth. The renaissance was accomplished slowly. All growing areas were charted for their days of ripening warmth, and soil condition. From one end of the state to the other, Dr. Maynard Amerine conducted planting and harvest testings. The finest vine species were correlated to optimum environment. The noble *Cabernet Sauvignon* of Claret, from Bordeaux, proved to be one of the best varieties for production in California. *The tonnage yield per acre would not be its criteria; the grape would become only the pride of premium quality wine growers* . . . as in France.

The search after Claret . . . among Americans . . . required marketing differentiation, eliminating the halting comparisons between the wines of Europe with alleged counterparts from California. A young journalist, wine-merchant from New York, Frank Schoonmaker, must be given the most credit for inaugurating a new nomenclature for premium California wines. Generic titles, borrowed from Europe . . . Claret, Burgundy, Sauterne, Rhine, etc., would guarantee nothing in the way of the wine's pedigree in California. But if the wine were to be called by the name of the predominating grape from which it would be made, the consumer could come to know the finer wines . . . made from those finer, shy-bearing, noble grape varieties . . . as the *Cabernet Sauvignon*.

The search after Claret . . . by you . . . for your table, to bring that joyous satisfaction of a good bottle of wine, is no longer difficult. Try any of these: Almadén, Beaulieu, Buena Vista, Christian Bros., Korbel, Inglenook, Krug, Llords & Elwood, Louis Martini, Paul Masson Souverain and you will not be disappointed. Hold a cellar supply one year, two years, three years . . . and you will magnify their merit . . . with bottle-age.

The search after Claret . . . for the connoisseur . . . requires a yardstick of qualitative judgement. Two thousand years have given the vineyards of Bordeaux a little edge over Californian vintners, and economic conditions are not the same. The five great Growths of Bordeaux . . . *Châteaux Margaux, Château Latour, Château Lafite-Rothschild, Château Haut-Brion, and Château Mouton-Rothschild,* are never inexpensive, and never unimpressive. The Classification of 1855, which ranked the leading châteaux of Bordeaux on the basis of their traditional market demand to that date, gave 2nd Growth listing to Mouton-Rothschild, a blow to its prestige which has only served to rank it apart, and today, above all the rest, for in the succession of direction from Baron Nathaniel Rothschild, in 1853, to the fourth direct descendant, since 1922, Baron Philippe has made of this estate, a monument of worthy pride. The labels bear the total pedigree of each vintage. Ten thousand people visit the cellars each year, as to a shrine. The Baron has gathered here, also, in a private museum, dramatically lighted, the tangible artifacts of wine in civilization. Since 1945, most bottlings carry, as a crown to the label, an original tribute by a contemporary artist . . . Jean Cocteau, Georges Bracque, Marc Chagall, Dali . . . *"Son tender velouté seduit les plus rebelles."* So reads the artist's inscription on the 1962 vintage . . . *"Its soft velvet seduces the most unfeeling."*

Château Margaux emerged from a long management of indifference, in the early 40's as the Ginestet family of Bordeaux took over the reigns . . . and with devotion, re-established the great name.

It is a long way from Julius Caesar's table in Rome . . . to yours and mine, but every one of the people in our cast of characters in *The Search after Claret,* as you and I, wanted only the wonderful satisfaction which comes from good red wine. How they got it, has been the history of our world, both the Old and the New!

Further proof that even the better cooks in ancient Rome made good use of wine, comes to us in the fragmentary notes of one Apicius, whose reputation for a good table was well known to his sovereign, Augustus. From those notes, we have tested this marinade for beef, which assures top sirloin, or even top round, the tenderness of a filet, when baked, roasted, or broiled.

Sirloin en Marinade

Marinade:

1 large carrot, sliced	1 bottle red wine
1 large onion, minced	1 cup salad oil
2 celery stalks, chopped	2 crushed bay leaves
1 clove garlic, pressed	12 juniper berries
½ teaspoon each: rosemary, thyme, oregano	12 peppercorns

80

2 tablespoons parsley, chopped
1 teaspoon salt

Cayenne pepper to taste
¼ cup red wine vinegar

Combine all ingredients of the Marinade; Simmer for a few minutes and cool. Pour over meat. Marinate for 12 to 24 hours in refrigerator, turning occasionally before cooking.

Roast:
3½ to 4 pound cut of Sirloin, or Top Round, cut as a Family Steak for carving in Chateaubriand style, in slices.

Drain meat from Marinade. Strain, and reserve liquid. Place meat on rack in open pan. Roast in 300° oven until meat thermometer registers 140°. Baste occasionally with marinade. Use drippings for Sauce, preferably non-thickened, but seasoned to taste.

Many a time, there's some red wine left in your glass, and some conversation to finish, and still no great desire for anything sumptuous from the pastry cart. French custom takes care of such moments . . . with permissible dunking of a very special kind of rich, molded sponge cake. Madeleines are individual, shell-shaped, and utterly delightful. The custom of dunking them in red wine comes from Burgundy, but even Claret, Chianti, or Cabernet takes to the treatment as a treat.

MADELEINES

1 cup sifted cake flour
3 large eggs, at room temperature
1 cup sugar

¾ cup butter, clarified and cooled
1 teaspoon vanilla extract
2 teaspoons grated lemon rind

Preheat oven to 400°. Sift cake flour and set aside.

Place butter in small deep saucepan. Heat slowly. Pour off clear butter from foam and sediment. Cool.

In the large bowl of an electric mixer, work eggs, sugar and vanilla together with a wooden spoon. Place the bowl over barely simmering water, stirring constantly, until the mixture is lukewarm. Remove from heat, and beat at high speed until light, fluffy, and creamy, and at least tripled in volume (5 or 10 minutes), incorporating as much air as possible.

Fold in flour, and lemon rind, gently. Stir in melted butter. Do not beat.

Brush Madeleine molds with butter generously. Flour. Spoon each shellmold no more than two-thirds full. Bake at 400° until light golden, or a tooth pick inserted comes out clean. This will take approximately 8 to 10 minutes. Time will vary between batches, as the mold and oven vary in temperature. Remove cakes from pans to cooling racks. Makes about 36 to 40 Madeleines. Store in tightly covered tins until used.

81

BURGUNDY

BURGUNDY . . . the bold music of the word draws the mind vigorously to a whole pageant of medieval imagery, echoing a turbulent history from Julius Caesar to Charlemagne and Napoleon, celebrating the glory of its wines beyond its kings and conquerors. Rudolph III, the last king of Burgundy, yielded the golden slopes of his vine-crowned domain to an ecclesiastical aristocracy almost a thousand years ago. The pride of the land was its wine. Vineyards nurtured by patient abbeys and soil-bound serfs, became the ransom prize for successive Dukes of Burgundy who treasured them as highly as their crown jewels. The wines of Burgundy were in short supply a thousand years ago, as they are today. An almost divine nectar of the grape, Alexander Dumas said it should be drunk "bareheaded and kneeling!" No other wine in the world is as rich in the tapestry of its definition, nor more universally imitated for the quality of its taste. The name is born of the region. Classic tradition defines Burgundy wine as the full-bodied, deep-hued champion of all the reds, of France, or California, South Africa, or Australia. Every wineland in the world today produces "Burgundy". It has no common price or common taste, the range of its quality being equally broad. It makes the task of finding the best examples more difficult, but the guide-lines to good wine remain constant, resting within the reputation of the grower and winemaker.

"Why," you may ask, "is a bottle of French Burgundy as high as $12. and a California Burgundy sometimes less than $1.? Is the French wine that much better?"

To the truly knowledgeable connoisseur, a vintage Romanée-Conti, Clos de Vougeot, Chambertin, Richebourg, or Musigny from a prime shipper is worth every penny of its price, as are the popular parish wines of Pommard, Beaune, and Nuits-St. Georges. Supply and demand keeps these internationally famous wines of Burgundy constantly in top price brackets. Supply is restricted both by weather and the limited acreage of planting. The whole vineyard region of French Burgundy is contained in 60,000 acres.

The bulk of the wine produced in any wine country does not compare with the small gallonage of its premium prestige houses.

Through all the centuries of wine-making, these have been the wines of ransom price, the joy of kings, popes and prelates, connoisseurs . . . and still are. The rest, for years, endured as *"vin ordinaire."* But the "whirligig of time" brings in many changes. Yesterday's thoughts about wine are as obsolete as treading out the vintage with barefeet! *In our own time, we are experiencing miracles of change, advancing quality in wines beyond the progress made in all the thousands of years since the existence of wine was first recorded!*

California seized the leadership of the world's wine industry following World War II, with technological advances obtained through close cooperation of the industry with the University of California Departments of Viticulture and Enology at Davis. Despite the fact that wine is, and since Noah has been essentially a product of nature, the application of the scientific method in an age such as ours has brought about tastable changes. Viticultural studies have produced new hybrid vine-stock, disease-resistant varieties. Micro-biology and enology brought forth ingenious new wine production techniques utilizing highly refined laboratory controls for watching and guiding the natural maturing of aging wines.

Elements of sunshine, rainfall, and the calendar's quota of warm weather alone produce, with the abundant wealth of our soil, the grapes which make the natural nectar. "The vine still her ancient ruby yields" but knowledge has improved with clonal selection, the canes on which the berries hang. The unpredictable nose of the cellarmaster has been bested by the constancy and reliability of instrument measures which note and tell the yet unhurriable process of change by time alone.

No single phase of the industry production has been overlooked, from growing to crushing, fermenting to bottling, from marketing to consumer education. Leaders of the European wine industry, today make pilgrimages to California to study this miraculous modern phenomena of product and marketing improvement.

It all began with the repeal of Prohibition. Vineyards and wineries which had been thrust into a deep sleep like the Princess in the legend of the "Sleeping Beauty" suddenly emerged, and awkwardly attempted to revive the commerce of yesterday. To reclaim a market, establish identity, and set itself apart from European competition and comparison, the race for quality of product began, bringing with it a system of labelling and wine nomenclature with parallel agricultural and wine-making techniques. Leading wines were named after principal grape varieties used in their production. These became known as *"Varietal*

Wines" . . . Pinot Noir, Cabernet Sauvignon, Semillon, Chenin Blanc, Gamay, Zinfandel, etc. To qualify for a Varietal label, a wine, by State regulation, had to contain a minimum of 51% of that grape. Simultaneously, wineries produced a program of "Generic Wines" named for the universally known regions of origin of those wine types, as Burgundy, Claret, Sauterne, Chablis, Rhine, etc. Imitation of European prototypes was not the goal then, nor today. Most winemakers in California had come from European wine countries. Here, in their own New World, they made wines as they did in their old homelands, to the best of their ability with the finest grapes available. With improved planting in California vineyards, the scope of the winemaker's art was enhanced by the greater abundance of Nature in the field.

Comparison, far from being odious, is primary practice for both winemakers and winelovers. It is a source of pleasure and intelligent awareness. From it, we may know the truth of the revolutionary remarks made in earlier paragraphs, leading to equally revolutionary and joyous news for the California wine consumer. No longer may the "vin ordinaire" or "vin de pays" be denegrated as something of minor consideration. The "wine of the country" in California, produced by top growers is unquestionably better than some of the best wines produced a generation ago, and far superior to much European export stock!

The "sleeper" of the market in California wine today, for the astute consumer, is to be found in the *generic* wines, and particularly *Burgundy!* Here, without limitation by regulation dictating the composition of the wine, the winemaker may blend grapes and wines to create the wine of his ideal. Just as an artist sees the picture in his mind before it is painted, so the winemaker approaches the wine he wishes to create. He wants his Burgundy to be mellow, round, tart or fruity, fragrant and full-bodied. In full freedom, he may blend to his ideal, limited only by the harvest of his fields. For this reason, the "Burgundy" of each winery will differ according to the talents, taste, and command of its winemaker.

Pinot Noir and Gamay are the principal grapes of Burgundy which give stature to the red wines of Romanee-Conti and its Côte d'Or cousins. Alone, as *varietal* wines in California, they rank among the best, commanding the highest price. But here is the tip to honest palates. Many a California *Burgundy* today rivals its *varietal* counterpart. For example . . . Buena Vista Burgundy is made of a blending of three *varietals* . . . Pinot Noir, Cabernet, and Zinfandel, a "secret" shared with me by owner-Frank Bartholomew. Paul Masson and Christian Brothers accent their Burgundy with Pinot Noir and artfully blend to obtain a round ideal with soft, deeper fragrance of other varieties. Ernest and Julio Gallo make use of the Petite Sirah, the grape brought to the French Rhone Valley by the Crusaders from the Middle East. Their *Hearty Burgundy* is a triumphant example of the qualitative improvement of product through its "Quality Control and Research Center" which employs 40 full-time wine technologists. It is a sobering realization of some awe to recognize that, in Gallo Vineyards, the revenues of size have been invested dynamically for the improvement of product. Equally stunning is the fact of enormous new vineyard plantings of premium vine-stock by Almadén with more than 4,000 acres at Paicines, and more than 2,000 acres equally devoted to premium wine production in new acreage by Paul Masson at their Pinnacles Vineyard in Monterey County. The status of *Burgundy* from Italian Swiss Colony's vine empire brought them medals from the State and County Fairs in 1966. Louis M. Martini, regarded by many as the Dean of California winemakers, has never hesitated to put his *Burgundy* to a taste-test-comparison with a French name contender. Old world, small oak cooperage aging softens Almadén and Charles Krug Burgundy. Supply and demand limit the availability of Beaulieu Vineyard Burgundy, but if you find it, buy it!

California Burgundy today is one of the best dividends of our abundant vineyards and applied intelligence in winemaking. There is nothing "ordinary" about our "vin ordinaire"! The best part of the boast . . . is the taste of its truth. Taste it in goblets instead of thimbles. Pour it chilled before dinner, if you like, in generous draughts, with a twist of lemon, and blend of conversation. Room temperature will release the full bloom of bouquet.

Ski buffs know there's nothing as cheerful as a steaming glass of spiced red wine as a welcome when the weather outside is icy! Here's a recipe with centuries of tradition to back up its appeal:

ARCHBISHOP

2 Medium-sized oranges stuck with cloves	½ cup of sugar
	1 bottle of California Burgundy

Stick oranges full of whole cloves and roast for 10 minutes in a moderate oven until oranges take on a golden brown color. Cut into quarters. Heat wine with sugar until thoroughly dissolved, *but do not let it boil!* Pour over orange quarters into pre-heated glasses, and serve with a fleck of nutmeg, with cinnamon sticks for stirring rods. Serves 8.

The kitchen value of California Burgundy far exceeds its modest price. A splash in most sauces, with every kind of beef roast, or chicken casserole lends particular magic. Don't be afraid of it, nor this classic French recipe for:

Burgundy Beef Stew

3lbs. beef stew meat	2 tbsp. cooking oil
2 tbsp. flour	2 cups beef broth
1 cup Calif. Burgundy	12 small white onions, peeled
1 bay leaf	1 8 ox. can pitted ripe olives
¼ tsp. each Sweet Basil Thyme,	1 small onion
Parsley, and ground Coriander	2 whole cloves
1 medium clove garlic	1 ounce Calif. Brandy
Salt and pepper	½ pound mushrooms, or tinned buttons
Meat Tenderizer	

Thoroughly moisten meat with water, and sprinkle meat tenderizer evenly, like salt over surfaces of the meat, piercing deeply with a kitchen fork, for penetration and to retain meat juices. Shake meat cubes in bag with flour until meat is coated. Brown meat in hot oil, or shortening, in skillet or heavy stew pan with a tight-fitting lid. Add garlic, herbs and spices, beef broth, onion stuck with cloves; cover tightly and bring to a boil. Reduce heat. Add red wine, onions, mushrooms, and simmer over low heat for 1½ to 2 hours, or until meat is fork tender. Just before serving, add pitted olives, and garnish with chopped, fresh parsley. Further garnish with glazed carrots, and green peas adds to the charm, as does, perhaps a final added splash of California Burgundy!

CHIANTI

THE BOOT OF ITALY has been full of wine for more than two thousand years. Long before there was a Roman Empire, six centuries B.C. those extraordinary folk, the Etruscans were making wine in the hills and valleys of what is known today as Tuscany, a region easily recollected pictorially from the pastoral backgrounds in so many paintings of Botticelli, Michelangelo, Titian, and Donatello. The green rolling hills are patterned with olive groves, vineyards, stately green-black fingers of cypress trees grouped like frightened figures, cathedral towers, and crenelated castles, all mingling in a landscape of classical beauty. This is the Chianti country, where Dante and Boccaccio wrote. It neighbors the hill-town of Assisi where St. Francis lived. It claims Florence and Siena in its cultural heritage.

But not only the Etruscans were making wine in the northern half of the boot, before the time of Romulus and Remus; the whole peninsula, from top to toe, flourished with the grape. The first colonizing Greeks named the country *Enotria*, Vineland. Today, Italy produces more than a billion gallons of wine each year. Much of it is so casually produced, and consumed, it scarcely deserves reportage. It's a blessing that most of it is also locally consumed. To find that small amount which is superb, the stuff inspiring poetic rapture, has been a quest of respectable citizens since the time of Augustus Caesar and his articulate chronicler, Pliny the Elder. Even that good wine is a matter for argument. The same quarrels about the merits of Soave and Valpolicella, or a rare little Barolo wine with the fragrance of wild violets and iris from Piedmont, take tempers high in winesmanship, when a lyric Latin tells about an amethyst-pink Caruso wine with the fragrance of lilacs grown on the terraced hills of Ravello. "It was the same wine that inspired Wagner to compose the celestial music of "Parsifal" when he lingered in the gardens of *Klingsor* along the Amalfi drive." It's useless to argue. The list of standard Italian wines counts more than a hundred names. The wines themselves vary from shipper to shipper, from cask to cask. We can do no better, by way of *apologia* for any omissions here, than to cite Pliny: "*I am aware that many of my readers will think that I have omitted a great many wines from my list, since each of them has his own pet choice and, wherever we go, the story about the Divine Augustus holds good. One of his freedmen whose palate and judgment of wine were absolutely first-rate was tasting some wines for the Imperial table, when he remarked on a local wine and said to the Emperor's host that its taste was certainly new to him and not of the finest. 'But,' he added, 'that makes no difference, for the Emperor will drink nothing else.'"*

Faking wine in Italy isn't new either! *Life Magazine*, in February 1968, ran a humorous exposé of the current national wine scandal, which has revealed that one-third of all Italian wines on the market, mostly inexpensive table wines, had never seen a whole grape." The ersatz wine was made from the dregs of *bona fide* wine, but "improved" as *"vino migliorato"* by the "sophisticators" as the swindlers were called, through the addition of beet sugar, potassium ferrocyanide, ox blood, and ethyl chlorocarbonate. Even Hollywood filmstar Tony Curtis joined the ranks of wine documentarians in a letter to Times-columnist, Joyce Haber: "Some of the big manufacturers were discovered making wine out of old water, banana peels, parts of rubber tires and everyday little things that you might find anywhere. It's a terrible dilemna for most of the Americans here," he continued, "We do all the wine drinking and we leave the driving to the Italians, which is the second mistake you can make in Italy."

The "old water" Tony Curtis referred to was really just well water. The "sophisticators" didn't dare use tap water. It would not only be too expensive, but metered, and the abnormal consumption could bring about investigation. Investigation, however, *did* come about. A special fraud police, the *Nuclei Antisofisticazioni* made some cloak and dagger raids, and caught the swindlers wine-red handed. Some of them quickly dumped hidden vats, with double-bottomed storage tanks. One cornfield was stained wine-purple for months, but the tanks were empty when the police arrived. But 110 "sophisticators" were caught and jailed. Six thousand were accused of "improving" wines, at 1,546 trials. One hundred and fifty million lire in fines were paid. That Italians in large numbers switched to beer and soft drinks began to show up in 1968 wine-consumption figures.

Just a few weeks ago, the Associated Press carried a story showing wine-consumption down from 147 quarts per year to 124. "Many Italians," according to the AP story, "don't seem to mind (adulteration), taking the view that the stuff looks like wine and tastes pretty good, so what's the difference? Others are worried. Some doctors are advising patients to lay off anything but high quality vintages for fear mysterious additives will cause gastric trouble. The popularity of beer as a meantime drink is rising among young people.

"Since July (1968) the Italian government has been busy prosecuting 188 persons said to have put out 50 million bottles containing a mixture of water, acids, sugar, and artificial coloring."

Ah, Œnotria! History only repeats itself. The reporter for the Divine Augustus was writing this about Italian wines in 69 A.D.: "*They have set up a regular factory, coloring wine with smoke and what is worse, adulterating it with noxious herbs and drugs. Dealers even use aloes to fake the taste and color of their wines.*" Even the richest Romans had a hard time getting good wine. "*Now not even the greatest can enjoy pure wines anywhere. Trade morality has come to such a pass that only labels and cellar names are sold, and the must is adulterated while it is still in the press. And the result is a strange paradox; the wine of least repute is least sophisticated and most wholesome.*"

Even Pliny experienced "sophisticated" Italian wines! His advice, however, remains timely. The complex of Italian wines still produces a "strange paradox." The knowing connoisseur in America, or even in Italy, *can* find wines of antique fame which are still pure, still as fragrant as violets, iris, and lilac, still as brilliantly beautiful as cut jewels, rubies and garnets, or golden yellow, blending to the haunting depths of amber. They come from time-honored vineyards and reliable shippers whose names are well-known . . . Bertani, Bolla, Fontonari in Venetia, Ricasoli, Antinori, Melini, Gancia, Ruffino, and Nozzole in Tuscany of Chianti. There is no reason to deny yourself the pleasure of Orvieto, Est! Est!! Est!!!, Lacrima Cristi from the slopes of Vesuvius, Barolo and Barbera and Asti Spumante from Piedmont, Marsala from Sicily, or if you can find it, Ravello Rosa, that Grand Caruso wine. Soave and Valpolicella do not have the full charm of their taste in Venetia; they suffer slightly in their voyage across the Atlantic. Notwithstanding this, they still have true distinction.

The most dependable and truest wine of Tuscany remains Chianti. If you've never tasted it except in a *fiasco,* the straw-wrapped flask, you haven't tasted the finest. The best *Chianti Classico,* from the delimited area between Florence and Siena, is never shipped in *fiaschi;* it is always bottled in the straight-sided, Bordeaux-type bottle, illustrated in our photograph. All genuine Chianti carries an easily recognizable seal, adopted by the Florentine Chianti League in the 14th century. That coat of arms shows a black cock on a gold field. Pre-eminent in the struggle to maintain the identity of true Chianti wine has been the austere and highly professional vintner of Brolio Castle, the Barone Ricasoli. "Brolio Riserva" a *Chianti Classico*, is always a vintage wine, aged from three to five years, tinged with copper in its garnet hue, truly fragrant with a curious recollection of field-fresh raspberries.

The Marchese Niccolo Antinori exports not only a *Chianti Classico*, Villa Antinori, a vintage wine, too, but delicious Orvieto, Bardolino, Valpolicella, and Soave, all under the elite Antinori label.

Should chance find you driving north one day on the old paving stones of the Via Flaminia, across the Pope's bridge over the Tiber, out of Rome, you will come to appreciate Italy as Œnotria...Wineland. You will believe the country produces a billion gallons of wine per year. Vines are everywhere. They are a part of promiscuous agriculture, which has vines growing between trees, *on* trees, growing in competition with olive trees, tomato vines, crowded into compact corners by postage-stamp wheat fields. This multi-crop system of the peasant farmer, follows no science, beyond tradition handed down from father to son. The wine made is for daily consumption with pasta, not an aesthetic experience upon which to make a studied critique. This is the bulk of those billion gallons of wine. The farmer would probably prefer his often gassy, poorly fermented wine to the refined product of classical vineyards. Taste is formed by habit. In the cellars of Brolio Castle, Barone Ricasoli has stored vintages reaching back into the last century. They easily establish what refined heights can be reached with the *Sangioveto* grape of *Chianti Classico*.

Nobody knows what kind of wine the Etruscans made. We only know their revels included wine in copious draughts, judging from the girth of the graceful black clay goblets, so prized today by antiquarians. Historians also know that amorous promiscuity was aided by the vine. Etruscan orgies made Roman banquets, or Hugh Hefner's dreams pale in comparison. Those 5th century B.C. citizens were waited on by naked slave girls, and feasted twice a day must sumptuously. Alas, only the ghosts of their culture remains. As a people, they were long feared by the Romans, who ultimately vanquished them. The taste of the Caesars was prejudiced against the wines of the area. Taste for the wines of Tuscany rested in limbo, among local farmers, until the 14th century . . . when true Chianti was born.

Musing about wine is never so delightful as when it is being sipped with a perfectly complementary food. The ideal companion for a *Chianti Classico* from Tuscany, or one of the California expressions of this wine-type from the Italian-born dean of California winemakers, Louis Martini, or the prize-winning San Antonio Winery Chianti, or that from Sonoma, of Sebastiani, or the Santa Clara Valley version of Almadén . . . is real, home-made egg pasta, *pasta all uovo*. Commercial noodles are universally available to make passable fettucine, with butter, cream, and fresh-grated Parmesan cheese, but for a memorable experience, try Tagliatelle, with that wonderful emerald-green, herb and cheese-fragrant *Pesto Genovese!* It will take time, but schedule it for a week-end when in-door pleasures are in order. If it's raining, or snowing, you won't mind being house-bound with Chianti and this pasta!

Tagliatelle with Pesto Genovese

For the Pasta:

3½ cups sifted all-purpose flour	1 tablespoon oil
5 eggs	1 teaspoon salt

Break the eggs into a deep bowl and mix them slightly with the oil and salt. Sift the flour into a large mixing bowl. Make a well in the center. Pour the eggs into this well, and work flour and eggs together with your fingers, slowly until it is all thoroughly combined. Work it into a ball, and place it on a lightly floured board. Knead it with both hands until it is firm and completely smooth. Wrap it in a clean cloth, dipped in warm water, and wrung out completely. Set the wrapped ball of dough aside to rest for half an hour, while you make the *Pesto*.

Roll the dough out very thin. You may have to divide it with a knife into two sheets if your working board is small. Lean heavily on the rolling pin, and keep on until the dough is almost thin enough to be translucent. Flour it lightly and fold it over upon itself several times, then slice it into noodles ¼-inch wide with a sharp knife. Unroll each slice and drape the noodles over a lightly floured, clean cloth.

Pesto Genovese:
(This is an adaptation, substituting parsley for fresh Sweet Basil, which is almost impossible to obtain generally.)

1½ cups very fresh parsley, stripped from stems, firmly packed into a 2-cup measure	1 clove garlic (through garlic press)
	¼ cup chopped walnuts, or pine-nuts, if possible
4 spinach leaves, washed, dried, minced	½ cup olive oil
1 tablespoon dried Sweet Basil	1 cup freshly grated Parmesan and
1 teaspoon salt	Romano Cheese
½ teaspoon freshly ground pepper	

Place all ingredients, except cheese, in a blender. Mix at high speed briefly, pushing herbs down with a rubber spatula. It will make a thick, green paste. Turn off the motor and add ½ cup of the cheese, blending just enough to mix thoroughly. Rectify seasoning with salt.

93

For preparation and service:

4 medium potatoes, sliced thin
4 tablespoons butter
2 tomatoes, peeled, seeded, minced

Put the sliced potatoes in a *very* large pot with plenty of slightly salted, cold water, and bring to a boil, having added 2 tablespoons of butter. When the potatoes are almost done, drop in the noodles, and cook until they are *al dente*. Drain . . . but save about ¼ cup of the cooking water.

Put the noodles and potatoes into a pre-heated serving bowl. Add butter and tomatoes, and the remaining ½-cup of cheese at once, along with the ¼ cup of hot water in which the noodles were cooked. Top with the *Pesto*. Present at table. Mix again and serve at once. The recipe will serve 6, memorably!

Chianti-land and California have more than wine in common . . . they have the artichoke! Lucky tourists in Rome may possibly be there in the season when baby artichokes are available . . . fresh. A few cafés will alternate their *antipasto* with *carciofi* . . . artichokes . . . in a dazzling variety of presentations. They come *con salsa al burro*, braised with bread-crumbs *alla Romana*, with chopped fresh basil and dry white wine, served on golden toast, with mushrooms in a *duxelle*, plus Gruyere cheese, with spinach . . . *Fiorentina*, or in a Lucullan formula with truffles and marsala! Each chef has his own way with *fondi di carciofo*, his own caprice with hearts of artichokes!

Highway Number One, which ribbons the California coastline from Morro Bay to Carmel, also runs northward through the fields of artichokes growing above Monterey in Castroville. In summertime, you can buy whole plastic-bagsful of tiny, baby artichoke hearts no larger than small plums. Should Fate give you this privilege, you may taste a souvenir of Rome . . . from your own kitchen. (Lacking the fresh, baby artichokes, the 5 to 7 count in 4½ ounce tins will do.)

Herbed Baby Artichoke Hearts-Romana

Wash. Remove stems and first few leaves. Clip points, and cut off the tops fairly far down, with a scissor. Then sit them in water, about an inch deep. Add salt, garlic, and a slice of lemon. Bring to a boil, and simmer slowly, covered for about 15 minutes. Drain. Remove all tough outer leaves (those that you can't eat whole). Slice through in half, lengthwise, then dip in this batter:

Herbed Dipping Batter

1 egg, slightly beaten
½ teaspoon Ac'cent
1 cup ice water
¼ teaspoon each: Basil, Sage, Thyme

1 cup sifted flour
½ teaspoon salt
2 tablespoons salad oil

Beat all ingredients together to blend. Heat salad oil in electric skillet to 400°. Drop artichoke hearts, dipped in batter, into hot oil, and simmer to pale golden, turning once or twice. Drain on paper towels. Serve with lemonaise, which is homemade blender-mayonaise made with lemon juice instead of vinegar.

PORT

*"... it makes the eyes quick to see, turns all things
fairer and brings back the blessings of sweet youth."*
Gaius Maecenas 64-8 B.C.

It might seem an anachronism to wax eloquently of the symbols of peace in a time of war, of the gentle life in times of violence, yet in this very process is a temporal cure, in the consideration of a certain wine, as an antidote for the soul's rebellion. Too often, in the unsophisticated minds of the young, Port is only a tonic for the elderly. If this be medical prescription, we might only say, *"How sweet it is!"*

The peaceful luxury of this velvet-rich wine contains an unmeasurable component we may call calmness. The curious connection of the palate with the mind can detect it, with a suggested command that makes it almost impossible to gulp Port in unthinking draughts. It is not the liquor for the toss-pot. It cannot substitute for any potable fire-over-ice. It is warming, but establishes that warmth with its own tempo, dictating the leisurely pace of philosophical contemplation. More than one solid scholar has been lead to call Port "the wine of philosophy." It demands, and produces, a mood which glides with ease into voyages of discovery ... in the time of Now. It calls a halt to fearful contemplation of tomorrow, or the sorrows and regrets of yesterday. It creates an eloquent Present, bringing you into sensory consciousness ... a liquid robe to cover you with instant solace and new strength.

How can a wine do all this? Look deep into the illustration accompanying these words. There you'll find Port's best companions ... cheese, walnuts, apples, the nibbling harmonies that dictate leisure and good talk. Tradition brings the decanter clockwise around the table at the conclusion of dinner, as a beginning to the substance of an evening ... the pace-setter for the train of thoughts which may ensue.

Before you make any rush to judgment, (for who hasn't tasted "Port") and put the paens of praise above to the likes of palates other than

97

your own, consider the broad range of quality in Port wine, which marks every step in the process that makes this wine from grapes. Here is no hackneyed history of loose round terms. The story must begin in Portugal. The wine takes its name from the Roman designation of the mouth of the River Douro . . . *portus cale*, or *the* port-Oporto. Britain and Portugal were bound together with the Methuen Treaty of 1703, strengthened by the earlier marriage of Charles II to Catherine of Braganza. Anglo-French relations cooled. Claret was heavily taxed and the taverns of old London served the wine of their new Queen's land. The new Treaty exchanged bolts of cloth from Britain for pipes of wine from Portugal. And so it was that from this ancient land of the Roman Lusitania, a strange ruby-red wine became a hallmark of British taste that still endures. Vintage, Tawny, Crusted, or Ruby . . . Port wine is uniquely delicious. Its liquoreuse substance reveals its richness when you swirl the glass, and allow its film of tracery to flow back into the bowl. These are the "tears" of the wine, sometimes called "legs" and most poetically referred to as "cathedral windows" when the flowing pattern breaks into arching rivulets.

The grape of Claret is Cabernet Sauvignon. Burgundy and Champagne boast of the Pinot. Riesling predominates along the Rhine. Palomino gives Sherry its identifying character. But there is no one single grape species growing on the Douro Bankside terraces. There are more than seventeen different species. The pride of their red varieties are various Tinta vines . . . Tinta Cao, Tinta Madeira, Tinta Carvalha, and one called Souzão for deep color. But you needn't remember those names. Remember only the process by which the juice of these grapes becomes the noble wine that has excited strong men for centuries.

Portugal is perhaps the one country left where the vintage is still a festival of barefoot pressing. Festival is an under-statement of the time. The whole countryside rocks with harvest celebration. Rockets are fired into the air carrying bundled twigs of dynamite, timed to blast in the heavens. Drums throb all along the vineyard-banks of the river where the *Gallegos* are trampling out the vintage in great stone rectangular tanks, almost filled to their three-foot depth. Whole troupes, as many as twenty men and women, arms locked, high-step back and forth in a ritual as formal as a quadrille, until every grape is crushed. And still the dance goes on, until the fermentation warms the wine. The *Gallegos* will have red legs for a month, but this night is all vigorous song and dance until the moment when the natural sweetness of the wine reaches a measured point where it must be drawn off, and brandy added, to arrest the fermentation.

Of course we don't have that kind of a festival in California, but the principle is the same . . . punching the cap of skins down into the fermenting wine to give color . . . watching, waiting, measuring sugar content until just the exact moment when the sweetness matches the winemaker's ideal. Several of our better California vintners imported Tinta grape species from Portugal sufficiently long ago to enrich our market with finer Port. These same winemakers also are quality-minded in choosing the brandy with which to marry the fermenting juice. All of these steps are quality decisions affecting the product as you pour it into your glass.

Tawny Port is aged in wood until it acquires a bronze edge to its crimson hue. Ruby Port is apt to be younger, bottled after two years in wood. Vintage Port is a blending of wines all of one year's making, bottled usually after two, or three, or more years in wood, at the judgement of the winemaker. Then it rests in its crystal chamber, making a pigment "chemise" on the walls of the bottle, known as a "crust." This patient ageing mellows the wine, and produces evidence of its transformation in an honest sediment, which falls to the bottom of the bottle. Before serving, it must be carefully decanted. As you pour it out slowly against the light of a candle, it runs like liquid jewels, with the promise of pleasure. These Vintage Ports, bred in the camellia-covered hills of Portugal are marked in British history. They are still being made . . . and you can find them here. For two centuries, one of the most famous names has been Dow. If you quest about, you'll find Dow's Vintage 1955 Port. It's been ten years in its bottle . . . and is a treasure of taste. And so is their Boardroom Tawny Port.

Tawny Port is always a blending of aged wines. "Port eats itself up," a Portuguese winemaker told me, "It's good just so long, then it goes down hill. It feeds on itself . . . so we add a younger wine to older blends." And here is where the art and skill of the winemaker comes into its highest degree of exactitude. He must know each of his components as a man knows his children and their differing personalities. He "marries" them in his blending to produce a wine that is dark, rich, supple as velvet, courtly in elegant texture. His cellar will have casks of wine, some more than twenty-five years old, or older, to lend particular character.

At every step of the way, there has been choice. The best wine is the result of the finest blending of the finest components, including the quality of the aged pot-still brandy. Esteem for our native wines will rise dramatically if you compare one of our best Port wines with an equally high-ranking Portuguese import. The experiment is an elegant kind of fun, and the group reactions of taste provokes even further explorations into what Samuel Johnson referred to as "the wild vicissitudes of taste." Your program should include, from California, one or more from these: Ficklin Tinta Port, Llords & Elwood Ancient Proverb Port, Buena Vista Vintage Port, Paul Masson Rare Souzão Port, Christian Brothers Ruby Port and Chas. Krug Tinta Madeira Port. Fine Port is also presented by the Novitiate of Los Gatos, Beaulieu Vineyard, Louis Martini, Weibel, and Almadén. Couple these in matching types with the illustrious Sandeman, Harvey, and Dow. The scan of your own discrimination will be broadened.

The pleasures of Port are not confined to its beverage service. There is an exquisite simplicity in this dessert suggestion:

FRESH PEACHES BAKED IN PORT
(Serves 6)

6 whole ripe Elberta Freestone Peaches	1 lemon — both strained juice, and rind
1 cup Port Wine	Fresh grated Nutmeg
1 cup sugar	1 ounce Cointreau

Plunge whole peaches, individually, momentarily in boiling water, to remove peel carefully with paring knife. Combine remaining ingredients, stirring over low heat to blend. Place peaches in a baking dish, and pour syrup over them. Cover. Bake in 400° oven, basting occasionally, until peaches are soft. Approximately 45 minutes or slightly longer. Chill. Serve with Almond Macaroons.

As an after-dinner conversation savory, to accompany heated walnuts, apples, pears, grapes and toast fingers, try this:

SAVORY CHEDDAR MOUSSE
(Serves 8)

2 packages (8 ounce) Cream Cheese	1 tablespoon Cognac
¼ cup sweet butter	¼ teaspoon dry mustard
8 ounces grated sharp Cheddar cheese	¼ teaspoon Worcestshire sauce
2 tablespoons heavy cream	

Allow all ingredients to obtain room temperature, or at least soft enough to blend, using either a rubber spatula, or better still, your fingers to whip the mixture until it is light and fluffy. Pile it sumptuously into a footed compote, and surround it with heated walnut halves, toast fingers. It may also serve as an appetizer, with raw cucumbers and radishes, as wafer background.

This small collection of suggestions on the service of Port wine would be incomplete without the classic winter weather recipe for:

Port Wine Negus

Pour the desired amount of Port wine into a glass or enamel-lined saucepan, and heat it slowly, not allowing it even to simmer. Add about one tablespoon of water per serving, a little lemon juice, and pour into heavy glasses, or heated mugs. Sprinkle with grated nutmeg, garnish with a lemon slice, with a stick of cinnamon as a stirring rod.

BRANDY

*Claret is the liquor for boys, port for men, but
he who aspires to be a hero must drink brandy.*
BOSWELL's *Life of Dr. Johnson*

IT IS TOLD of M. Charles Maurice de Talleyrand, 18th century Europe's most renowned gourmet, how once, at the conclusion of one of his feasts, when a champagne brandy of great age and distinction was served, one guest took up his glass and downed the liquid in a quick gulp. The celebrated host, not unmindful of his position, was startled into perceptible amazement.

"Oh! my dear sir!"

"What have I done, Monseigneur?"

"Well, sir, since you ask me, let me tell you that a fine champagne of that age and quality deserves to be appreciated."

"Doubtless, Monseigneur, but I am one of the uninitiated."

"Well, sir, one can learn . . ."

"With pleasure, Monseigneur. Would you vouchsafe to instill the first rudiments?"

"Willingly," replied Talleyrand, "Thus: one take's one's glass in the hollow of one's hand, one warms it, shakes it and gives it at the same time a circular movement, so that the liqueur may liberate its scent. The one lifts it to one's nose, one breathes it in . . ."

"And then, Monseigneur?"

"And then, sir, one puts the glass down, and . . . one talks about it!"

There is much to talk about . . . to the novice, and the initiated. What is this fragrant essence, sometimes called the "soul of wine"? How is it made? How did it all begin? Where? When? Why is it known, in the *Materia Medica* as *aqua vitae*, and to the French as *eau de vie*? Why is it sometimes like searing fire on the palate, and yet, on other occasions, a mellow, comforting balm?

The conversion of gentle white wine into what one of Dr. Johnson's contemporaries called "liquid fire and distilled damnation" brings into focus the art and science of distillation, with that curious dichotomy, which since ancient times, has made the product both boon and plague. Intelligence and reason can dismiss the latter. Shakespeare posed the problem in *Othello* . . . "*O God! that men should put an enemy in their mouths to steal away their brains!*" . . . and within the same scene, gave his answer, in the words of *Iago*, to stand for all time: "*Come, come; good wine is a good familiar creature if it be well used; exclaim no more against it.*"

In balanced judgment, and use, brandy has had therapeutic use for more than a millenium. The science of distillation was known to the ancient Egyptians. Centuries before Christ, the Chinese made spirits from rice wine. Aristotle, the great Greek philosopher left written record that their golden age knew the secrets of extracting spirits from wine. The modern history of distillation still goes back more than five hundred years, to have veiled origins. The word "alcohol" is Arabic, and so is "alembic" the name of the vessel into which source-wine would be placed for firing . . . as a still. A tenth century Arabian alchemist, one Albukassen, was not able to turn base metals into gold, but from wine he made a potable spirit he called *uisgebeatha* — meaning "water of life." Italians claim the art of distillation was invented by Arnand de Villeneuve, born in 1238, in Spain, and as Arnaldus Villanova was educated in Sicily, and then taught medicine, astrology and alchemy at Avignon and Montpellier. As one of the most erudite men of his day, the first man of record in science to make brandy, it was he who introduced it to the *Materia Medica.*

Out of the Dark Ages of the alchemist, science emerged; an essential principle was revealed. Alcohol vaporizes, becomes steam, at a lower temperature than water. The boiling point of water is 212° F., when it becomes steam, or vapor, while that of alcohol is 176° F. If heat is applied to wine, or other alcoholic liquid, and the temperature is kept below 212°, all of the alcohol may be separated from the original liquid. If, in the same process, an apparatus is used to collect those alcoholic vapors, and not allow them to escape into the air, it is possible to re-condense them into liquid form. The result is a crystal-clear liquid, colorless alcohol of high purity . . . the distilled soul of wine.

According to a contemporary expert of the brandy world, those primitive pot stills, using only a round-bottomed copper pot, a hood with a long taper-neck, and a coiled, worm-like condenser to pass through a barrel or jacket containing cold water for assisting the rapid condensation of the vapors, are not only still in use, but, with minor improvements, the best kind of still for making the most potable brandy. The vapors rising from the fired alembic, or pot still, are captured in the hood, and by gravity, flow through the cooling spiral which transforms the vapor into liquid. In the Cognac area of France, there are about 7,000 distillers, small farmers who distil their own wine in one single little pot-still. These are the findings of many famous names in the Cognac trade.

All Cognac is brandy, but not all brandy is Cognac. This is merely one vineyard area of the world, about 140,000 acres, where brandy production had a great and good early impetus. The wines of this area, about 70 miles north of Bordeaux, had acquired considerable fame in the 16th century, not so much because of their quality, but from the ease of shipping from their nearby Port of La Rochelle off the Bay of Biscay. Foreign ships found it easy to traffic in barrels and casks of the local wine. Then along came the 100 Years of War, with consequent blockades, creating surplus, and over-production for the almost non-existent market. According to legendary history, a Dutch apothecary visiting in La Rochelle, was moved by the plight of the farmers, and discussed with them, the possibility of "burning" their wine to "extract the heart." This, he told them, would take less space to store, and incidentally, to ship. And so it was that the farmers of the Cognac district began to distil their wine. The Dutchman called this miraculous spirit "Brandjwyn", meaning "burnt wine", moving into our language, the Anglicized word . . . *Brandy*.

All of this sounds very, very simple. Take wine, put it into a copper still, fire it up, condense the vapors, and lo, and behold, . . . brandy! But it takes time and science to make, from this "distilled damnation" a mellow, potable beverage. Twentieth century ability, within laboratory analysis, has allowed us to fractionate the physical and physiological characteristics of not only the component elements of brandy, but the separate alcohols, aldehydes, furfural, esters, acids and other constituents which are the composition of brandy. We can know the effect of age . . . in wood, in glass, of air and oxidation. We know, by organolpetic examination and laboratory analysis how much of the perfume and flavor derives from the soil in which the grapes were grown. Better wines make more palatable brandy. If a vineyard has been sprayed with free sulphur dusting during the growing season, or sulphur dioxide added to the must during fermentation, it may persist in the wine, and become even more apparent and obnoxious in the distilled product. Wines fermented at high temperatures will yield a brandy that in itself is less than perfect.

"Fine brandy begins with fine wine," according to Otto Meyer,

105

President of Paul Masson Vineyards, and one of the world's leading experts in brandy production, a position to which he comes from many generations of his forebears in Europe. "In the distillation, all of the component elements, the aldehydes, higher alcohols, known collectively as 'fusel oil', become part of the product. For *fine brandy*, you want to retain the *perfection of the wine* . . . keep the desirable, and eliminate the undesirable. This requires a skillful operation, with highly sophisticated methods of distillation, demanding all the technical skills and knowledge of an engineer, with quality control by test analysis. From these finely distilled brandies, one can then build up an inventory, with age, in wood, for blending to an ideal." He reminded us that it was that jovial Californian, Paul Masson himself, who said that brandy was "the only drink distilled from something good to drink." Whisky is distilled from malted grains, a fermented mash of zero sensory appeal. Brandy begins with a fine wine, and owes the complex pattern of its final golden bouquet to that attar of wines. Ten casks of white wine produce one cask of brandy. One drop of brandy left in a glass, may leave its perfume for days. Rubbed, as experts do, between the palms of the hand, that single drop will be a rare essence. In sophisticated, thin crystal balloon glasses, warmed by the palm, there is, indeed, something to talk about, as those separate components rise and mingle, and repeat, each address like the notes of a Bach fugue.

What makes a good mellow brandy? The source of the distillate, age composition of the still, its operation (French farmers in the Cognac region actually sleep with their stills, tending the fires with special wood), careful age in wood, and final blending, and reduction to marketing proof . . . 80°.

That term "proof" . . . really doesn't make much modern sense, semantically. It's an English term, derived long ago to measure the potable strength of the beverage. It was tested with gunpowder. Mixed in equal amounts, and then lighted with a flame, if it failed to burn, the spirits were too weak, if it burned too bright, it was too strong, but if the mixture burned evenly, with a blue flame, it was said to have been "proved." That potable mean today, we know was 50 per cent alcohol, by volume, which is 100 proof. Each degree of proof is equal to one-half of one per cent alcohol. Ergo, a 90° proof beverage contains 45 per cent alcohol. The ideal for beverage brandy, and the standard for Cognac, is 80° proof. Fine California brandies are also 80°.

It is erroneous to believe that a 100° proof spirit makes a better drink. This hang-up of some people probably originates in the notion that a whisky or brandy which is "bottled in bond" carries some benign approval of the Government. Uncle Sam is only there to collect a tax on the spirits as they flow from the still! Actually, he could care less about the sophistication of its quality. Government regulation does require beverage brandy to have four years of age in wood, but even the least expensive brands on the market exceed this minimal requirement. The best have a large percentage of components of much greater age.

In the seventeenth century, it was found, in Cognac, that surplus brandies, resting in oak barrels, mellowed and improved and took on an increasingly golden hue year by year. Some houses began to differentiate their brandy with stars, and others with letters. V.S.O.P. would mean Very Superior Old Pale. For all of his historic significance, Napoleon's name on brandy means absolutely nothing today. The quality of French Cognac, like any other brandy, is determined by the source of the distillate. Wine grown in calcareous clay soil, from Folle Blanche grapes, produces superior brandy. The heart of the Cognac region is known as the *Grande Champagne,* so called because of its similarity of soil composition to the region where Champagne is grown. The surrounding areas are subdivided by the clay composition of the soil, into seven classifications: Grande Champagne, Petite Champagne, Borderies, Fins Bois, Bons Bois, Bois Ordinaires, and Bois Communs. Look first, not for stars, or initials, but for the source. All of the brandy from the greater district may be called "Cognac" but that from the Grande Champagne is the finest.

While the Cognac district of France leads the world in its reputation for brandy, it cannot claim all the laurels. While some Spanish brandy that got on the market too young and raw evoked the jest of "Franco's revenge", the highly sophisticated Fundador from Pedro Domecq, distilled from Palomino grapes, from the spirit that is the backbone of Spanish Sherry, is truly unique. The Greek Metaxa, carries a hint of the resin in its dark, and soft touch of sweetness. Another is flavored with anise; this is Ouzo, mixed with water, as an aperitif, becoming a milky, opalescent hue. One hundred years ago, in California, after the gold rush, Pisco Punch from Peru had knock-out fame. It was merely what it is today, a grape brandy shipped from the port of Pisco, Peru, matured in porous clay jars. In Peru, you may sip it at high proof, but the export is reduced to more potable proportions.

How does brandy become 80° proof? It flows from the still, when made well, as it is in the golden perfection of modern knowledge and equipment in California, at 160° proof, into bond. It is taken out of bond, and reduced, with distilled water to 100° proof, for aging, in

50-gallon white oak barrels. Universally, uniform coloring is given with burnt sugar, or caramel. Nothing else, but age, is added. The highly technical skill of a master-blender attends to the rest. All of the better California brandies, — Paul Masson, Christian Brothers, Almadén, and Korbel, come to market at 80° proof . . . mellow, smooth, aged, masterfully blended. Each has bouquet, body, dryness, lightness, smoothness, and flavor.

Brandy-making is not new in California. The Mission Fathers made it from crude pot-stills in the 18th century. The captain of Fort Sutter gained some fame from his distillery in 1843. Governor Stanford's vineyard at Vina produced the prestige brandy of that *belle epoch* around the Bay area.

The rush to market every kind of wine and spirits following the repeal of national prohibition in the United States, brought many imperfect products to the public palate. The subtlety of fine brandy was not universally understood; the still seemed a unique way of salvaging poor wines, and stretching the use of pressed grapes, by distilling pomace, as the French make *marc*, and the Italians, *grappa*. Quality-minded consumers took refuge in 100-proof, bottled-in-bond spirits. Such brandies are seldom potable. Happily, those days are gone. Time has brought understanding to our operation of both pot-stills, and more sophisticated column-stills. Premium wineries, decades back, planted Folle Blanche, Colombar, and Saint Emilion grape varieties especially for delicate wine-source material for brandy, as in France. Time has also given us mature blending inventories, aged in oak. The increase in public acceptance of California brandy, doubling in sales-volume with each decade, suggests that the distinctive identity of our finer product has achieved its own niche, in full and open comparison with French Cognac.

The greatest amount of credit for the mercurial rise in popularity of American brandy is owed to Christian Brothers, who, in the early 40's pioneered the market with the first soft and sophisticated brandy on the market since Repeal. It is still a leader in the field, and one of California's finest products. In the same quality field many an after-dinner snifter is a lingering pleasure from pourings of Korbel or Masson's mellow spirit.

In all brandies, taste-quality, beyond price, is what the customer is seeking. It is always a prestige spirit.

Brandy for heroes? It would be presumptive to define the Boswellian "hero" . . . as either a cardboard lover, or a brave idiot. He is more apt to be the ordinary man with sufficient courage to face his own reality. Winston Churchill was such a man, and brandy was his drink. A 19th century writer defined brandy as "a sovereign remedy in almost all the disorders of the human frame." A 20th century text has amplified that appreciation: "It is the greatest medium known for the purpose of permitting man to forget, at least for a little while, the shortness of life and the ludicrously helpless and infinitesimal part he plays in the functions of the universe."

BRANDY: Suggestions and Savoir-faire

After-Dinner Service: Any thin crystal, stemmed glass, with a bowl of tulip-shape, which can accomodate the warming palm of the hand, and capture the bouquet, may serve as a *snifter.* Oversized balloons are frequently awkward and unnecessary.

Flaming with Brandy: It is the volatile fumes rising from warmed brandy which ignites, not the liquid itself. Too much other liquid in sauces, is apt to dilute, and extinguish flames. Cold brandy added to a hot pan will ignite almost instantly. Be wary of flaming dishes containing oil or grease; a conflagration will result. Steaks, omelets, roast chicken, crepes, and poached fruits — apples, peaches, pears, take on more glamorous appeal and flavor, when warmed, flaming brandy is poured over them, in a chafing dish, before serving. Indispensible for Cherries Jubilee, and Crêpes Suzette. Superb blended sparingly with equal parts of sweet butter and Roquefort, as a dessert cheese to spread on thin, melba toast triangles.

Drinks made with Brandy: Tall drinks; Brandy & Soda, Brandy Collins, Fizzes, Rickeys. Cocktails: Old-Fashioned, Manhattan, Brandy Sour, Stinger, Alexander, Side-Car, Gimlet, French '75. Flips, Nogs, Punches: Indispensible in most recipes, including the holiday Egg Nog, Tom & Jerry. Café Brûlot, Café Royale, and Cappuccino owe their forte to Brandy.

Cappuccino La Scala

Almost inconspicuously off one of the main intersections of Beverly Hills, California, is Jean Leon's celebrated *La Scala* restaurant, an in-spa for top-flight Hollywood celebrities, and famed lastingly for another of its most loyal patrons, the late John F. Kennedy, for whom one of its most sumptuous private dining rooms is named. Young host, Jean Leon lives today on the crest of his enthusiasm for wines, which keeps him on a jet-commuter schedule between California and Spain, where he has a castle with a vineyard, where he makes wine, not as a dilletante, but an enologically oriented *amateur des vins,* which, in

French parlance, means one who really knows the score about wines. The cellar at La Scala, originally the first bank vaults in Beverly Hills, today hold a new kind of wealth, a six-figure inventory of the finest wines of two centuries and two continents. There is no price on the Château Lafite Rothschild 1889. "It is sold," Jean allows, "only by the caprice of my desire to part with it, which is not easily persuaded, by money, which can be more quickly replaced."

There are few men who combine poetic ideals with financial acumen, enlivened with youthful vigour. Jean Leon is one of these. His formula for *Cappuccino*, that punctuating froth of hot coffee homogenized with live steam, has long been a trade secret, guessed at by many, and known by only a few. If you have one of those expresso machines which is equipped with a steam jet, you can make it correctly. If not . . . follow the trail to La Scala. The proportions here will depend upon the size of your a.d. coffee cups. It begins with 2 regular-size cups of coffee, to which you must add:

1 tablespoon coffee cream	2 ounce jigger fine Brandy
1 teaspoon Ghirardelli Ground Chocolate	2 ounce jigger of combined Rum, Grand Marnier, Cr. de Cocoa

The listed ingredients, together, are a "mix" to add to coffee, which in turn, is injected with live steam, until it is a volume-increased frothy brew. Enjoy!

The culinary uses of Brandy could make a whole book, one chapter of which would be devoted to Desserts, flamed with Brandy, or merely flavored with this "soul of wine." Far and away the most famous of all flaming desserts is Crêpes Suzette, French pancakes, quarter-folded, swimming in a sweet orange syrup laced with a trio of brandy-rich liqueurs, all blue-blazing in dramatic presentation at table.

The late Henri Charpentier, whose final days were spent presiding over a bungalow hide-away rendezvous for gourmets, in Redondo Beach, with his devoted assistant Marie, is usually given credit for the creation of this dish, in the mauve decade, on the French Riviera. Some say a dining room subordinate lackey clumsily jostled the elbow of the young and handsome Chef Henri as he was preparing the pancake dessert at tableside for the current favorite of the Prince of Wales, thus setting the skillet of volatile sauce alight. Having known the memorable Chef for many of those later years, with profound respect for his culinary knowledge, gained from a lifetime of service that began with apprenticeship in his teens, it is not probable that an accident had anything to do with the classic recipe's origin. He knew that heated Brandy was volatile, that those fumes were highly flammable from kitchen training, that only the essential flavor of a liqueur would remain, once the alcohol would be burned away. It is classic treatment for many roast chicken recipes, the understanding known for the addition of wine to sauces, and computed even as to minutes in loaning the final filip to soups before service. No, it is not likely Crêpes Suzette, nor their flames were an accident. The visible combustion of invisible fumes, into sudden bright flames, dancing over food in a darkened dining room brings fascinating sorcery to any dish so subjected, from a spinach salad to a chocolate sundae, lifting the ordinary to epicurean status.

The menu of the Beverly Hills Hotel has listed, for years, a rich, dark chocolate fudge sundae, named for Gertrude Lawrence. It is merely thick chocolate fudge sauce, heated in a chafing dish (over very low heat in the blazer pan) blended with Brandy poured in a blazing steam at the finish. Poured over vanilla ice-cream, it makes a deliciously rich and spectacular finish to dining. With several additions, it became a favorite on the menu of the memorable Tirol Restaurant, in Idyllwild, under the appropriate title of

Glace Vanille au Chocolat-Bigarade, Flambé

In the blazer pan of a chafing dish, ladle the desired amount of prepared Chocolate Fudge Sauce. As chocolate scorches readily, keep the flame low. Once the burner beneath is lighted, stir constantly. Add several tablespoons of chopped toasted almonds, and over the pan, grate one whole orange. Stir, to blend. With a long-handled Brandy ladle, lower the cupping end, filled with 2 ounces of Brandy, to the flames, having momentarily removed the blazer pan of chocolate sauce to one side. Pass the heated Brandy through the flames. It will catch fire instantly, if it is hot. Replace the blazer pan, pour the burning Brandy into the sauce, stir, until the flames subside, and ladle over firm vanilla ice cream.

Crêpes Impromptu

Recipes for Crêpes Suzette are too commonly found to need detailing here. The argument about *the* recipe will go on for years, *sans chic*. The idea will persist with infinite variation. Even Chef Henri made his own. Experienced cooks know that sugar caramelizes with heat, and makes a syrup, with the addition of butter and liquid. So . . . heat brown sugar, with butter, add orange juice (or even use orange marmalade, with natural pectin to give substance), simmer, and reduce, and you are ready to receive, in the Suzette pan, crêpes, to bathe, fold, and put aside in quarters. Liqueurs? Brandy, of course, Triple Sec, Curacao or Cointreau (for orange flavor) Grand Marnier, and/or Rum! The moment the liqueurs are hot, pass a spoonful beneath the blazer, through the flame, bring the burning spoon into the pan. *Voilá!* Your own Crêpes Suzette!

In Spain, much ceremony is made in elegant dining rooms, with the service of an orange. Gloved waiters are skilled in peeling, with a knife, the glorious fruit, in one long, unbroken spiral peel. With none of the white membrane showing, the speared orange is lowered to a plate, deftly sliced, each glistening wheel spread in overlapping circles like cards, and presented. In a chafing dish, such sliced oranges, with diagonally cut slices of banana, in the same brown sugar-orange juice-butter-liqueur syrup, become an instant Ambrosia, Merely fold the crepes over a slice of banana, top with orange slices, and finish with a garniture of toasted coconut, and you have *Crêpes Valencia!*

You may have your own recipe for Crêpes, but if not, here is one to begin with. Try it several times, and I assure you, you will evolve your own formula. The addition of Brandy helps to make the edges crisp and lacey. The handling of the skillet in flipping the delicate cakes, is dexterity which comes only with practice.

CRÊPES

2 eggs	1 teaspoon salad oil
½ cup milk	½ teaspoon Brandy
4 tablespoons flour	¼ teaspoon salt

In a medium-size bowl, combine all ingredients and blend with a wire whisk until smooth. For each crepe, melt ½ teaspoon of butter in a 7-inch skillet. Pour in just enough batter (about 3 or 4 tablespoons) to cover the bottom of the pan, by quickly rotating the pan. Cook over medium heat until lightly browned on the under side; turn and brown the other side. Stack crêpes on a plate, and keep warm in a low oven. The recipe makes about 10 to 12 pancakes.

INDEX OF RECIPES